YOUR
COMPETENT
CHILD

Toward a new paradigm in parenting and education

First published in the United States by Farrar, Straus and Giroux
First american edition 2001
Revised edition by Balboa Press 2011

Visit the author's Web sites:
www.jesperjuul.com
www.family-lab.com
www.zentv.se
http://twitter.com/#!/family_lab
www.facebook.com/familylab

Balboa Press books may be ordered through booksellers or by contacting:

Balboa Press
A Division of Hay House
1663 Liberty Drive
Bloomington, IN 47403
www.balboapress.com
1-(877) 407-4847

Because of the dynamic nature of the Internet, any web addresses or links contained in
this book may have changed since publication and may no longer be valid. The views
expressed in this work are solely those of the author and do not necessarily reflect the
views of the publisher, and the publisher hereby disclaims any responsibility for them.

The author of this book does not dispense medical advice or prescribe the use of any
technique as a form of treatment for physical, emotional, or medical problems without
the advice of a physician, either directly or indirectly. The intent of the author is only
to offer information of a general nature to help you in your quest for emotional and
spiritual well-being.In the event you use any of the information in this book for yourself,
which is your constitutional right, the author and the publisher
assume no responsibility for your actions.

Printed in the United States of America

ISBN: 978-1-4525-3890-7 (sc)
ISBN: 978-1-4525-3892-1 (hc)
ISBN: 978-1-4525-3891-4 (e)

Library of Congress Control Number: 2011915546

Balboa Press rev. date: 09/27/2011

Contents

Acknowledgments

The theories and many of the examples used in this book arose from my work at The Kempler Institute of Scandinavia in Denmark. To Walter Kempler, M.D., and the other staff members of the Institute, my sincere thanks for their inspiration and for their unfailing confidence in me during the many years when I had little confidence in myself.

My thanks are also due to the many families from all over the world who let me into their personal and private lives. I recall with embarrassing clarity my attitudes and prejudices upon meeting many of them for the first time—those from Japan and Islamic countries, families of mixed ethnic origins in the Croatian refugee camps, and American families ravaged by alcoholism, to name a few.

My grown son, now 37, has helped me to integrate my experiences in a way that can be done only by someone who is openly and honestly searching for his own life. The same applies to my wife, whose very existence confronts me with what I hope each time are the last remnants of my childish self-centeredness.

Preface to 2. Edition

When the 1'st edition of this book was published I had the feeling that many societies around the globe were well on their way to establish more healthy and constructive relationships with children and youth and between adults as well. Today I'm not convinced that this is happening, although there is tons of good will supporting such efforts.

With my knowledge of parents and other adults living and working with children I had expected that our societies would welcome their "competent children" and celebrate their competence and feedback. To a great extend this happened within families. Although many parents found it difficult to transform their inherited ways and roles many succeed and discovered an abundance of hidden treasures in their co-existence with children.

Among teachers, counselors and others working with children something else happened. They felt not only provoked but also disrespected by the competent children and sometimes even by the very fact that children are indeed far more competent than they were led to believe in their educations and trainings. Many started dreaming and talking about the "good old days".

This has raised a basic question which all of us must find our own answers to: What do I want?

Which are the human and social qualities that each of us would like to see in our children/pupils/students when they turn twenty? For me, with my profession in mind, I would like to see young adults with a strong and durable mental health and solid psychosocial competences, none of which are disturbing academic or creative achievement. On the contrary they are enhancing these efforts and aspirations.

I actually believe that most of us would like to see that – parents, teachers and politicians as well as pedeatricians, grandparents and neuroscientists. In relation to this objective the so-called good old days as well as a lot of contemporary attempts to raise and educate children were disastarous. You only need to take a look at your national statistics for: alcoholism, drug abuse, crime, mental illness, domestic violence, child abuse, rape, school-drop-outs, eating disordens, suicides and suicide attampts, bullying and a whole bunch of behavior digagnoses, over-consumption of prescription drugs and dependencies to realize this. All these phenomenon are not only causing collosal human suffering but the sheer costs of trying to treat, prevent and control them have reached levels that we can no longer afford.

The past two decades of cinical as well as pedagogical praxis has convinced me that only by adopting a new paradigm will we be able to develop in healthier ways. This paradigm is already available if we combine the experiences and know-how of the most successful families with all the evidence from the new developmental psychology, attachment theory and the findings of neuroscience plus thousands of successful projects around the globe. We know what to do. All we need to learn is *how* to do it. I hope that reading this book will feel as a incentive to begin or go on whatever you current position might be.

Jesper Juul

Familylab International

Introduction

Like so many people my age, I knew when I was in my twenties that there was something wrong with the way in which my parents' generation (and the generations before them) looked upon the structure of the family and the raising of children.

In the course of the decade that followed, as I trained to become a family therapist—working with so-called maladjusted children and young people, and with groups of single mothers—I realized that my attitudes about families and child rearing were neither better nor worse than those of my parents. In fact, our thoughts had the same fundamental weaknesses. First, they lacked ethical substance. Second, they were formulated according to an arrogant and polarizing assumption: some people are right, because they act in accordance with the right attitudes, and other people are wrong, because they act in accordance with the wrong attitudes.

This tendency to polarize was also inherent in the feedback I received from my colleagues and clients. Some of them thought that I was good at what I was doing; others didn't. In my naïveté I thought that as long as the first group was in the majority, I was safe. It took some time before I realized that I should have listened to those from the dissenting group. This didn't happen until I became a father and experienced my own lack of competence. That's when my education began. Until then, I'd only been in training.

Before I became a father, I believed that families should be characterized by understanding and tolerance, and that relationships between parents and children should be democratic. This approach was in direct contrast with the moralizing, intolerant, and controlling type of upbringing that I knew was destructive for children's self-esteem and vitality.

But as I spent time with my son, and through my everyday work with families with children, I began to realize how superficial my attitudes were. Granted, our understanding of the role of children in family and society has changed in many ways from what it was when I was growing up. Our grasp of human nature, our means of punishment, and our attitudes toward educational and public morality have all become more humane and less restrictive. Yet I became aware of two factors that challenged and pained me both professionally and personally.

As a teacher and supervisor, I saw firsthand, all too often, that parents were struggling. They would meet with therapists to discuss their children, and they would leave the meetings feeling like losers—less able to take action and more inadequate than when they arrived. And the therapists with whom they met also left these meetings feeling helpless and incompetent. Yet bound by duty, they clung to traditional clinical psychology, which is more concerned with finding fault than it is with identifying possibilities.

As a family therapist, I saw that children and young people still had to bear the brunt of this disconnection. We still saddle children with a responsibility that few parents, politicians, educators, teachers, or therapists are willing to take upon themselves. We are not motivated by ill will; on the contrary, we love our children and believe that they need to shoulder this responsibility in order to grow. But our logic is flawed. Our fundamental understanding of what kind of beings children are is mistaken.

The Swedish psychologist Margaretha Brodén has expressed this idea in a single sentence that has provided the inspiration for the title of this book: "Perhaps we have been mistaken; perhaps children are competent?" (Mor og barn i Ingenmandsland/ Mother and child in no-man's-land, Copenhagen, 1992).

Brodén's insight arises from the scientific context of her work and from her special interest in the early interaction between infants and their parents. Because I am a practitioner and not a researcher, and because my area of experience is the interaction between children and adults in the broadest terms, I have a slightly different perspective on her observation.

In my view, we have made a decisive mistake by assuming that children are not real people from birth. Both in the scientific and the popular literature, we tend to regard children as potential rather than actual beings, as asocial "semi-beings." As a result, we assume, first, that they need to be subjected to massive influence and manipulation from adults, and second, that they have to reach a particular age before they can be regarded as equals and real people.

In other words, adults have to find ways in which to bring up children so that they learn how to behave like real (that is, adult) human beings. We have identified certain methods of upbringing and labeled them along a spectrum, ranging from "permissive" to "authoritarian." Yet we have never really stopped to question the validity of the assumption.

This book questions this assumption. I believe most of what we traditionally understand by the term "upbringing" is both superfluous and directly harmful. Not only is it unhealthy for children, but it also hinders adults, precluding their growth and development. Furthermore, it has a destructive influence on the quality of relationships between children and adults. By perpetuating instead of questioning this principle, we create a vicious circle that also interferes with our understanding of education, rehabilitation, and social policy regarding children and families.

Thirtyfive years ago, my generation played a part in creating an illusionary distance between "me" and "society." This was a logical extension of our clash with authority. Yet it has persisted over the years and has become increasingly dangerous, particularly when coupled with the fact that politics have been reduced to economics in the meantime.

It is perhaps more true now than ever before that the way in which we behave toward our children will determine the future of the world. Our access to information has increased to such an extent that we cannot assume that our two-faced attitude regarding raising children will remain undetected; that is, although we preach ecology, humanitarianism, and nonviolence when it comes to world politics, we treat children and young people violently.

For several years now, I have had the privilege of traveling and working in different cultures. My travels have convinced me that the ways in which the relationships between children and adults have changed in the Scandinavian countries might serve as a model for other countries.

Visitors to these countries may see adults acting toward children in ways that, on the surface, seem spineless, confused, and irresolute. But beneath the surface, these relationships contain the germ of what can only be described as a quantum leap in human development. For the first time in the modern age, adults are seriously considering the inalienable right of the individual to personal growth from a nondogmatic and nonauthoritarian standpoint.

For the first time, we have a basis for believing that each individual's existential freedom does not constitute a threat toward the community, but is rather vital to the continued health of the community as a whole.

The way adults and children relate to each other varies greatly.

There are huge differences between families in Asia, Europe and America, but also within each of these continents as well: families in northern Europe differ from those in the south, and those in the former Eastern Bloc. There are even distinct differences between regions in the same country. Naturally, a country's culture, political history, and religious beliefs play an important role in a nation's self-awareness. Foreign visitors tend to notice these beliefs. I overhear immigrants in Denmark say that they do not want their children to be like Danish children, yet Danes are easily outraged to see how physical southern Europeans are with their kids.

These differences are difficult enough to deal with on their own, but the trend, particularly in the United States and in many European countries, is toward the creation of multiethnic, multinational societies. I believe that it is important to be able to see beneath these culturally determined styles. The social importance of the family varies from one culture to another, but its existential importance is the same. The pleasure we derive from constructive and healthy interaction—and the pain caused by destructive relationships—is identical no matter where we live, even though it may be expressed in different ways.

Throughout this book, I will contrast the "old" with the "new," not to criticize the old, but to identify concrete possibilities for action. In my everyday work with families and mental health professionals, I have seen that many parents are very open about their attitudes. Deep down, they know when they act inappropriately, but they are unable to change because they need tangible suggestions. Yet because the type of interaction I am proposing is so new, there are as yet not many role models.

Traditional clinical psychology often questions people's emotions: How much do parents love their child? How much does a son hate his father? How angry is a daughter with her mother? These questions are important in that they allow people to express real pain. But I would like to underscore the fact that I have never met parents who have not loved their children, or children who have not been attached to their parents. I have, however, met many parents and children who are unable to convert the loving feelings they have for each other into loving behavior.

For the first time, we are ready to create genuine relationships that bestow equal dignity on men and women, and on adults and children. Never before in the history of mankind has this happened on such a large scale. The demand for equal dignity also means openness and respect for differences, which in turn means that we must abandon many of our impressions about what is generally right and wrong.

We can no longer just replace one "parenting" method with another; we can no longer continue merely to modernize our mistaken assumptions. Together with our children and our grandchildren, we are literally staking out new territory.

The anecdotes and examples suggested in these pages are meant to inspire individual experimentation. In other words, they are not meant to be slavishly copied. Parents are not just people of different gender; they are human beings who have joined together having had completely different experiences in their family of origin. Yet they also have much in common. We have all learned, as children, that there are different ways of entering into relationships with other people, only some of which are fruitful. As we come together to create a new family, we have the potential to learn what we could not learn in our first family.

When I say that children are competent, I mean that they are in a position to teach us what we need to learn. They give us the feedback that makes it possible for us to regain our own lost competence and help us to discard our unfruitful, unloving, and self-destructive patterns of behavior. To learn from our children in this way demands much more than that we speak democratically with them. It means that we must develop a kind of dialogue that many adults are unable to establish even with other adults: that is to say, a personal dialogue based on equal dignity.

I would like to clarify my position on a few key points before beginning. First, the fact that each and every one of us must find our own way of doing things—a way that is most fruitful for both ourselves and our children—does not mean that everything is equally good or that "anything goes." Throughout this book, I will refer to specific central principles, which individually and collectively form the criteria by which we can all judge our own actions.

I often refer to historical practices because I believe that the best way for most people to understand themselves and their actions is by using history as a mirror.

Finally, I am concerned that some readers will feel criticized by the ideas contained in this book. We live in an era in which we are quick to identify victims and assign guilt; consequently, many of us have a tendency to feel criticized. But this is not my intent. If you are satisfied with the way your family lives together and the quality of your relationship with your kids and with their development, there is no reason to change your ways.

FAMILY VALUES

We are at a unique historical crossroads. Across many different societies, the basic values that secured the foundation of family life for more than two centuries are undergoing a period of disintegration and transformation. In Scandinavia, women have been in the vanguard of these changes, abetted by advanced social legislation and the comforts of the welfare state. In other countries, civil war or economic hardship has sparked this development.

The pace at which change is occurring varies, but the cause is the same: the hierarchical, authoritarian family, headed by either a matriarch or a patriarch, is becoming extinct. The map of the world is teeming with many different types of families. Some make a desperate attempt to maintain the standards of "the good old days," while others experiment with new and more fruitful ways of living together.

From a mental health vantage point, there is every reason to welcome this change. The traditional family structure and many of its values were destructive for both children and adults, as these scenarios will illustrate.

A Café in Spain

A father, mother, and two sons, ages three and five, have just finished eating their ice cream and cake. The mother takes a napkin, spits on it, grasps the younger son's chin firmly, and begins to wipe his mouth. The boy protests and turns his face away. She grabs hold of a handful of his hair and tells him in an angry whisper how naughty he is.

His big brother looks on, grimacing—but only for a moment. Then his face settles into a neutral mask. The father also has a pained look, but then he turns with irritation toward his wife— Why can't she make the boy behave himself! Why does he always cause such a fuss?

By the time they leave the café, the boy has recovered. Window shopping, he notices a new toy in a store window and points to it enthusiastically. He wants his mother to look. But she is ahead of him, and when she walks back to him, she grabs his arm and whisks him away without even glancing at the toy in the window. He begins to cry, begging her to look at it, but she is unrelenting in her determination to win. "Pontela cara bien!" ("Make your face beautiful!") she repeats, over and over again.

A Café in Vienna Two young married couples, one with a son about five, sit down outdoors to have a cup of coffee after shopping. When the waitress appears, the boy's mother says to her son, "We're having coffee, what do you want?"

The boy hesitates a little and says, "I don't know."

Irritated, the mother says to the waitress, "Give him some apple juice."

The coffee and juice arrive, and after a while the boy says, politely and cautiously, "Mommy, I would rather have Coke with lemon, if that's possible."

"Why didn't you say that to start with!" the mother replies.

"Drink your juice!" But in the same breath, she says to the waitress, "The boy's changed his mind. Give him a Coke with lemon, so we can have some peace!"

For about ten minutes, the boy sits quietly while the adults chat. Suddenly the mother looks at her watch and says angrily to the boy, "Drink your soda!"

"Are we going?" the boy asks, visibly excited.

"Yes, we've got to hurry home. Now drink up!"

The boy swallows his Coke in large gulps. "I'm finished now, Mommy," he says happily. "Wasn't I quick?"

The mother ignores him and begins talking to the other adults. Once again, the boy sits quietly. After half an hour has passed, he asks cautiously, "Mommy, are we going home soon?"

"Shut your mouth, you little brat!" she explodes. "Another word from you, and you'll go straight to bed when we get home. Do you understand!?"

The boy withers and resigns himself. The other adults look at the mother with approval, and the boy's father lays an affirming hand on his wife's arm.

A Bus Stop in Copenhagen. A grandmother and two grandchildren—a four-year-old boy and a six-year-old girl—are waiting for a bus. The boy tugs at his grandmother's coat and says, "Granny, I have to go to the toilet."

"You can't go now," she replies. "We've got to get home!"

"But I need to go, badly!" the boy says.

"Look at your big sister, how big and sensible she is," the grandmother says.

"Yes, but I need to . . . really bad!"

"Didn't you hear me? You can go to the toilet when you get home. If you don't behave yourself, I'll have to tell your mommy. And then you won't come into town with me again!"

The adults in these scenarios are not bad people. They love their children and grandchildren, are delighted when the children behave themselves, and appreciate their funny and cute comments. But these adults behave in unloving ways because they have learned to regard unloving acts as loving, and loving acts as irresponsible.

For several hundred years, what we really taught children was to respect power, authority, and violence—but not other human beings.

The Family As A Power Structure

For centuries the family has existed as a power structure in which men have absolute power over women, and adults have power over children in terms of all the social, political, and psychological aspects of life. The hierarchy was unquestioned: the man was on the first rung, the woman below him—if there were no adolescent sons—followed by sons and then daughters. A successful marriage depended on the woman's ability and willingness to submit herself to her husband; the clear purpose of child rearing was to make children adapt to and obey those in power.

As in all other totalitarian power structures, the ideal was a situation in which no open conflicts occurred. Those who didn't cooperate met with physical violence or found their already restricted individual freedom further limited.

For those who understood how to adapt themselves, the family provided a secure foundation, but for those whose individuality was more robust, the family and its pattern of interaction could be alarmingly destructive. Those who suffered and developed symptoms were treated—by educators and psychiatrists—so that they would quickly readapt to living within the power structure.

When those in power (spouses and parents) tried to "resocialize" women or children who acted out, they were encouraged to show understanding, love, and firmness—but never to surrender their power. As a result, many women and children were admitted and often readmitted to institutions and forced to take medication.

Of course, this description is both incomplete and unfair. Admittedly, there were aspects of traditional family life that were pleasurable and happy. People loved each other. On another level, those who submitted successfully enjoyed a special form of security similar to that experienced by well-adjusted citizens in totalitarian societies.

Some of us may even feel nostalgic for "the good old traditional family," but only rarely did it exert a positive influence on the well-being and development of the individual. In other words, from a social point of view, traditional families often looked successful, but the pathology they caused lurked just below the surface.

Only toward the end of the last century did we begin to take an interest in children as individual beings. That's when we realized that meeting children's intellectual and psychological needs was important for their well-being and development. Recognition of women's rights came even later—in the 1920s—when women began to demand to be taken seriously as human, social, and political beings. Thus in the first half of this century, the family gradually became less totalitarian, although the actual power structure, which was the foundation of family life, remained unaltered.

One of the legacies of the traditional family exists in our language, which originated during a time in which successful families were defined as conflict-free, and when our ideas about what constituted a healthy family were vastly different from what they are today. I'd now like to update the definitions of many of the terms and concepts that we use when we speak about families and children.

Definitions

Methods of Upbringing

In Scandinavia we discussed methods of child rearing with great confidence right up to the middle of the 1970s. We believed that children were asocial and potentially animal-like; therefore adults had to associate with them and use "methods" that would ensure children's individual and social development. The methods varied along ideological lines, but the notion that it was necessary to use a "method" went unchallenged until very recently.

Now that we know that children are real people from birth, it is absurd to speak of "methods." Think for a moment about how we would sound if we applied this concept to adult relationships. Imagine, for example, a man saying to a friend, or to his therapist, "I'm in love with a tall, black-haired woman from Portugal, but I have many problems with her. Can you give me a method so that she will be less difficult to live with?" Clearly, no adult would think of approaching another adult with this idea in mind. But this is how we have approached our relationships with children since the beginning of the eighteenth century.

When children are born, they are fully human—that is, they are social, responsive, and empathic. These qualities are not taught, but are inborn. Yet for these qualities to develop, children need to be with adults who behave in ways that respect and model social, human behavior. To use a method—any method—is not just superfluous but also destructive because it reduces children to objects in relation to those who are nearest and dearest to them. It's time, according to both clinicians and researchers, to change how we relate to children—to move from a subject-object relationship to a subject-subject relationship.

The Age of Defiance

Around the age of two, children gradually begin to free themselves from their total dependence on their parents. Suddenly they discover their authonomy – a discovery that they litteraly celebrate by saying "no" to everything you say or ask. With a delighted smile on their faces they say "no" and the message is, "Look, I'm not you anymore! I'm ME – is'nt that wonderful?" They don't say no to oppose thier parents. They want to be able to think, feel, and act on their own. There's never any doubt as to when this independent age begins. One morning, as you dress your two-year-old daughter, she tugs at your arm and says, "Me can!" or "Me do it!"

And how do most parents respond? They say, "Stop it! You can't do it. I have to. We haven't got time to play games!" In other words, when children become independent, many parents become defiant!

Yet this brief anecdote also illustrates how clever children are at cooperating! If a parent meets his two-year-old's burgeoning independence with reluctance and defiance, the child will, in the space of a few weeks, become either defiant herself—meeting defiance with defiance—or lose her initiative entirely and become even more dependent.

Young children necessarily become increasingly independent and self-reliant—it's part of their development. Only a totalitarian system would view the natural and progressive development of a child's unique personality as a problem. Describing children as "defiant" is a typical ploy of those in power; it's intended to keep the children subordinate.

In this age your child is taking his or her first steps toward their individuality and if you as a parent enter into a powerstruggle with your child a lot of valuable energy is wasted and you might be installing a experience in your child, that will become evident when he reaches puberty.

PUBERTY

Puberty is a neutral clinical concept that has, over the course of this century, acquired an extremely negative connotation. Conflict, argument, and trouble—these are the qualities associated with adolescence. After World War II, the equally negative concept of prepuberty emerged—alerting parents of younger children to the fact that trouble is just around the corner.

Viewed objectively, puberty is an intrapsychic (that is, it takes place within the individual), psychosexual period of development that causes many twelve-to-fifteen-year-olds to experience internal uncertainty and turbulence. The idea that this development should in itself cause interpersonal conflicts with adults is rubbish. The number of conflicts and their intensity depend, among other things, on the ability of adults to acknowledge their changing parental roles, and on the way in which they approached the development of their child's integrity during the first two to four years of the child's life.

If for instance parents were engaging in numerous powerstruggles when the child was around two it's more than likely, that this child will enter puberty heavily armed. Back then he learned that if you want to develop your individuality in this family you have to fight for it!!

Teenage Rebellion

Similarly, the teenage years are described in militaristic, political terms: rebellion, independence, revolution, and lack of discipline. This is not surprising. In a power structure in which adults represent stability and are invested with maintaining a conflict-free environment, every progressive development must necessarily be defined as an attack on the establishment.

The same dynamic exists with women in midlife. When they begin menopause, their every action and mood is attributed to "hormones." This excuses those in power (men) from shouldering any responsibility for disruptions that arise. In the same way, teenagers are blamed for being teenagers. What adults need to do instead is face up to their overriding responsibility in terms of structuring the interaction within the family.

Now, let's consider a number of concepts we traditionally use in connection with child rearing that reflect how those in power view reality. Embedded within these concepts is the belief that maintaining the power structure is best for all concerned.

Setting Limits

Within a power structure it is necessary to have law and order; therefore, in the past, limits were set to govern children's physical, mental, and emotional pursuits. These limits—what children could and couldn't and should and shouldn't do—were enforced as if the family was a policing unit.

This system led adults to assert that certain limits were healthy and good for children—a proposition many people accepted, although there is no evidence to support it. Let me elaborate: It is true that children develop in harmonious and healthy ways when the adults of the family set some limits. But, as I will explain later, it is important that both children and adults set their own limits. The question of setting limits for others is first and foremost an expression of power.

The question of limits inevitably arises whenever parents discuss children's upbringing. We tend to think that only our generation has difficulty setting limits, that our parents accomplished this task with more ease. In fact, setting limits has always been difficult. Parents have always asked experts for advice about how to get children to "respond" or "obey," as they used to call it. For as long as families sought to uphold the power structure, parents were advised to think about setting limits in terms of four elements: unity, firmness, consequences, and fairness. Let's explore each of these in turn.

Unity

"Unity is strength," as the saying goes, and that was precisely the reasoning behind one of the family's most important credos: "It is important that parents agree about how to bring up children." I have met countless couples who sacrificed their marriages in order to live up to this ideal, and who suffered from overwhelming guilt because they did not succeed. They believed, as many parents do, that children feel the most secure when their parents agree, and that they were harming their children when they failed to agree. A certain amount of disunity was tolerated—but only if it was expressed after the children had gone to bed. When children were present, nothing less than unconditional unity was demanded. Yet this article of faith is true only if we insist on thinking of the family as a political unit. When those in power have to enforce law and order, it is to their advantage to agree, so that they can face their children as a united front.

Parents also perceived that disunity would allow children to play one parent off against the other—to drive a wedge into the family's leadership. Yet in practice parents seldom agree. For example, in many families dads dole out discipline only to have moms intervene for more leniency. In this situation, mom is viewed not as a disloyal soldier but rather as the family's first-aid dispenser whose job it is to tend to the wounded. Yet even as they performed this role, many women never questioned the necessity of setting limits, or thought to examine the confines under which they themselves lived.

To me, it is not important whether parents agree about upbringing or not. In principle, they need only agree about one thing, namely, that it is acceptable to disagree. Only when their parents experience each other's differences as wrong and undesirable do children become insecure.

Firmness

Firmness, which is related to unity, is also believed to be necessary to keep the power structure intact. When members of a family voice different opinions, the discord is experienced as hostile op-position, and creates conflict. What does it mean for adults to be firm? They have to be able to say, in unison, "NO!" when children disobey.

The healthy alternative to this power play is open, personal dialogue that takes into account the desires, dreams, and needs of children as well as those of the adults. To act in this way is to display true leadership.

Consequences

Suppose children still did not obey, even after both parents spoke with a united and firm voice. What next? Regardless of the particular conflict, parents usually select one of two consequences: either they resort to physical violence, or they limit children's personal freedom.

Neither of these consequences is easy to carry out. Most of us cannot physically hurt our children or restrict their personal or social freedom with a clear conscience. That's why we resort to these familiar justifications:

- "It's for your own good!"

- "You'll understand when you grow up!"

- "You must learn to adapt yourself!"

- "It hurts me more than it hurts you!"

- "If you won't listen, we'll have to knock it into you!"

- When a parent says, "I make the decisions here!" children learn to submit or rebel

  When a parent says, "Children should be seen and not heard!". Children learn that they have no freedom of speech, and that they need to censor themselves.

Interestingly, after punishing their children, many parents begin to worry that they have harmed their relationship with them. Typically, parents then express this fear as a demand—"Give your dad a hug now, and let's forget all about it"—or, more indirectly, as a question—"Are we friends again?" Ironically, this is what adults often say to each other when breaking off a loving relationship: "Can't we still be friends?"

These feelings of awkwardness and doubt are justified. By dealing in consequences and punishment, parents gradually destroy their relationship with their children. They decline all responsibility for the conflict that has arisen and turn the child into the guilty party. This pattern of treatment erodes not only the child's confidence in his parents, but also his own self-esteem.

The term "consequense" has become a softer synonym for punishment and the explanation usually is that it is necessary or even healthy that children learn that their actions and behavior has consequenses. In my experience punishment is neither necessary nor healthy and therefore it is a good idea to destinquish between punishment and what we might call *natural* consequenses.

"If you cannot sit still at the table you will not get any desert!" That is a punishment

"If you eat any more icecream you will probably get a stomachace". That is a natural consequence

FAIRNESS

For many parents, a large part of child rearing was concerned with criticizing and correcting children when they acted incorrectly. Children, then, needed to admit to having done something wrong, or demonstrate genuine remorse. According to this model, adults are responsible for making children recognize that they were truly and seriously in the wrong. Only after they admit that they were wrong can children begin to improve themselves. This way of thinking gave rise to such well-known expressions as

- "Shame on you!"

- "You should be ashamed of yourself!"

- "Aren't you ashamed of yourself?"

Under this system of child rearing, in which any conflict between parents and children can be explained by the lack or failure of a child's upbringing, the concept of fairness was introduced as a guideline for those in power. Practically, it allowed adults to ascertain that the child was truly guilty before the punishment was carried out. Thus parents didn't focus as much on the violence they would mete out, but on the unfairness that would ensue if they punished a child who was in fact innocent.

Paradoxically, because their parents operated on this concept of fairness, children often only remembered (and protested against) those episodes for which they had been punished for something they had not actually done. The more general—and deeply un-just—experience of being "wrong" was repressed, because it was normal—that is, it was the normal state of mind for children raised under a system in which criticism was considered the cornerstone of their education and upbringing.

The concept of fairness also surfaced in those families in which parents made a great effort not to treat their children "differently." According to this way of thinking, children—regardless of how dif-ferent they were—should receive the same gifts at holiday time, the same rewards, the same punishment, and the same upbringing. As a result, some children received what they really needed and some didn't—it was a toss-up. But parents could rest assured in the knowledge that they had been "fair."

The set of values I have described, emanating from an antiquated understanding of the nature of children, is still widely practiced in many parts of the world. Regardless of what one may think of this system of upbringing, we have to admit that the methods are highly correlated with success, or at least they used to be. Yet the goal—to raise children who behave—is insidious. It's summed up in a warning my friends and I heard innumerable times when we were growing up: "Now remember to behave yourself so that other people can see that you've been brought up properly!"

Our parents' priorities were based on this external value—that children learned how to "get on," "behave nicely," "fit in," "speak properly"; and that they say "Thank you," "How do you do?" and "Thank you for having me." Children were not supposed to be themselves. They were expected to "act," precisely as one acts in a play. And just like actors, they were expected to learn their lines.

Years later, knowing so much more about children than our parents did, it is easy for us to be wise. We need to remind ourselves that those parents who still cling to the notion of the family as a power structure do so because they honestly believe that it is best for their children. They do not experience this system of upbringing primarily as an expression of power.

THE DEMOCRATIC INTERLUDE

About twenty-five years ago, when my generation reached reproductive age, we began thinking of families in new ways. It was the dawn of a circumscribed period of time during which families tried to

restructure themselves according to democratic ideals. Much of the change was spurred on by the women's movement. After centuries of suppression, women wanted real equality. The ensuing struggle was about changing sex roles and reapportioning responsibility within the family, and about the inequality that existed in society with regard to employment and education.

Although many of us had grown up in families whose power structure had been more or less totalitarian, we felt that families needed to become more democratic. We believed that children should have the right to an explanation of the norms and limits imposed on them by adults. We also believed that children had rightsto contribute to and influence family decision making.

These precepts caused men and women, and adults and children, to interact in new ways. For example, parents demanded fewer methods of upbringing. Instead, they wanted to understand children and young people. At the same time, sexual relationships between men and women were enriched because women were making decisions about their own bodies. This was abetted by the drug industry, which made effective contraception widely available. During this time, the rhetoric was highly politicized.

This noble experiment, though valid, proved insufficient; that is, it had only a limited impact on reshaping traditional family values. Why did it come up short? During this period, families turned to political definitions to describe the problems that existed between the sexes and between adults and children—a logical and necessary intermediate step. But this political vocabulary cannot adequately describe internal family relationships. In fact, when used in this way, ideology tends to prevent rather than promote feelings of family closeness. Both ideology and totalitarianism provide a sense of security and meaningfulness for the initiated, but this security never trickles down to those at the bottom of the hierarchy, or to those who have a different perception of reality.

The Process of Family Interaction

Because of the hierarchy that exists within families, democratic values, while undoubtedly a healthy supplement to basic family values, are not, in themselves, sufficient. Be-lieving that everyone has a right to participate in decision making is helpful when we relate such participation to the content and structure of family lifesuch as deciding where to spend Christmas vacation this year and who will be responsible for which chores. But this approach does not affect the actual process of interaction, which is vital to how the members of the family feel and how they get along during the Christmas holiday.

The process of interaction, which we sometimes refer to as "tone," "spirit," or "atmosphere" (the Greek philosophers called it *Ethos*), refers to the quality of the exchanges between the people in a family: how they relate to each other and how they feel. It is the decisive element for the physical and emotional health and development of both children and adults, and it is influenced by many varied factors: the personality and life experience of the parents; their mutual relations; their individual ups and downs; their overview, perspective, and philosophy; their awareness of conflicts and their ability to handle them; their ability to be resourceful during times of stress and crises; their health; their social and economic circumstances, and so forth.

It is a psychological fact that the adults in a family are solely responsible for establishing the quality of this ethos or tone. They can neither delegate this responsibility to their children nor share it with them. Children simply cannot handle this particular responsibility. They need the adults to take the lead and if they don't everybody is in trouble.

This does not mean that children do not influence the process of interaction in the family. quite the opposite. They exert great influence by virtue of their lack of life experience; their logic; their handicaps, if any; and their sensitivity regarding conflicts combined with their lack of experience in resolving conflicts. They also influence the process through their desire to cooperate, their vitality and creativity, and because they often function as lightning rods for conflicts between adults.

Nevertheless, children cannot be responsible for the quality of the interaction. In families in which the parents, for various reasons, cannot cope with the responsibility, and in which the children end up "making the decisions," the result is always destructive: for the adults, the children, and their relationship. Tasks, duties, and practical areas of responsibility can be delegated to children and young people, but not responsibility for the family's well-being: that belongs to the adults.

This does not mean that children should be denied the right to influence decisions in a democratic sense. They can participate if the overriding purpose is to initiate them into the rules of democracy. In situations where children and adults have to function together, it is better for children if the adults take the wishes and needs of children seriously. In the family and in society as a whole, there is often an enormous and crucial difference between getting one's way and getting what one needs.

A family is only a judicial unit when it is launched and when it is broken up. Between these events, it is primarily an existential and emotional unit. We all do well when we respect each other's rights, but this respect is not sufficient for children's well-being and development. Healthy children demand more than equality in a political and judicial sense; they demand to be treated with personal dignity as well.

The transition described between totalitarian and democratic families resulted in a series of clashes that left many people wounded on the battlefield. But this change took place during optimistic times: we believed that the future would prove our efforts worthwhile. We wanted to dispense with the "old" without any clear idea of how the "new" should be characterized. To this day, many parents of our generation still regret that the "modern family" has not yet evolved to the point where it can solve its own problems.

Overall, however, democratic principles were soon shown to be of limited value when applied to real life. Too abstract to act as guidelines in everyday affairs, they proved more difficult to enact than to conceive, as I will now explain.

CONFLICT

To traditional families, the absence of conflict was an ideal. Consequently, when conflicts between adults and children arose, the parents were blamed for failing to bring up their children correctly, or children were blamed for their lack of good manners. As a result, the first generation of democratic parents was simply without role models and did not know how to negotiate and resolve conflicts constructively.

Naturally enough, these parents turned first to a political model— that is, to the struggle for power. But this model is unsuitable for families because it unavoidably ends with a loser and a winner. In families based on this model, family unity loses out. It's no wonder that divorce and one-parent-families have become more common than ever before in history.

Equality

In democratic families, the concept of equality manifested itself first as an attempt to abolish the old sex roles and remold them in a more equal fashion. These families wanted to erase the assumption that men were providers and women were housewives.

But many families—especially those that effectively equalized the roles of the sexes—needed to face up to an unpleasant reality: although "equality" was perhaps a noble goal both practically and organizationally, it did not create a healthier balance between men and women in other areas. As old stereotypes fell, others took root. Sharing the practical chores related to home and children did not solve the problem of how to divide emotional responsibilities and other issues related to family management.

Because men were the direct successors of the old totalitarian rulers, the role of men in the family was subjected to massive criticism. A great number of men experienced this criticism as a kind of castration. Yet there was a paradox coiled at the heart of the criticism directed at them: men as fathers had never played an important role (apart from the ver important role of providers) within the family, neither quantitatively nor qualitatively; subsequently, they were criticized mainly for what they did not do.

More or less obligingly, many men assumed more tasks and responsibility within the family at the same time that women began entering the job market. Taken together, these phenomena ended man's role as sole provider. Both men and women began demanding that men define themselves as partners, lovers, fathers, and family members – i.e. active participants in the emotional infrastructure of the family.

For a short while, equality was defined as "equal likeness," and the virtues of the "soft man" were extolled. Soon thereafter, the pendulum swung to the other extreme, and the "macho man" was celebrated. That's when both men and women realized that "giving women what they wanted" would not in itself create a more democratic family. The socalled feminine values, which for the main part are basic human values, could not be grafted onto men.

For thousands of years, women have been denied basic human rights, yet they have managed to maintain, to varying degrees, their human qualities. Men, isolated in their provider role and often abused at work, have distanced themselves from their human qualities. In that sense, the lack of equality is still conspicuous.

RESPECT AND ACCEPTANCE

Both "respect" and "acceptance" were key words in the new equality between the sexes, but both words are ambiguous; that is, they can be understood in highly distinctive ways, depending on who is speaking.

For example, is respect something we human beings ought to have for each other simply because we exist, or is it something that we have to "earn"? Should I respect my partner's way of doing things (the way she brings up our children, for example), or should I wait and evaluate the results?

Suppose my partner says, "You have to accept that!" Should I conceal my disagreement? Should I agree or act as if I do? Can she "demand" my acceptance? Or is it a gift I can give her because I love her? What happens if I respect her and accept her the way she is, but I realize that I cannot stand living with her? Is it necessary to understand another person before you can respect and accept him—or perhaps love him? Or is such an understanding superfluous?

To render these abstract concepts in concrete terms so that they can be helpful as we try to understand family life, we must first focus our attention inward. We must learn to accept ourselves as we are. This is how we acquire a de-gree of self-respect. Through this process, we learn how absurd it is to take it personally when other people disrespect us. Yet this brings us back to the starting point: are respect and acceptance prerequisites for love, or consequences of it?

Jesper Juul

Demands

Making "demands" is relevant when we speak of commerce, legal contracts, and political power games, but not when we speak of families. It is possible for a woman to demand that her divorced spouse pay child support, but not that he take responsibility for or pay attention to their child. A loving relationship between a man and a woman or between parents and children is a gift and a privilege. It is not something we can demand from each other.

When a family member demands something—whether it's responsibility, affection, regard, sex, attentiveness, duty, being together, or respect—it is inevitably a demand for love. It's a legitimate longing—but an absurd demand.

Yet family life is strewn with demands. Sometimes we are lucky enough to get what we ask for. But all too often we achieve our end at the steep price of losing contact with the person we long for.

For all these reasons, the attempt to remake families in a democratic mode is a step forward—but it has not been an entirely successful undertaking. It omits one dimension of family life that is essential to the good health and development of its members—dignity. The concept of treating people with equal dignity has existed in political manifestos for two centuries, although it has rarely been practiced. Similarly, it has been difficult to apply this concept to family life because we have so few role models and clear examples.

A Community of Equal Dignity

Relationships between adults and children have been improving decisively and qualitatively in the past twentyfive years as the concept of equal dignity within family life has emerged. This change is perhaps most clearly illustrated by the fact that children and young people are now able to function in the world with a much greater sense of naturalness and self-awareness. They are no longer automatically programmed to tolerate the infringements and violations inflicted by parents and adults that earlier generations were forced to accept.

At the same time, however, both the family and society still fail to fulfill a crucial need of children and young people: to see them—and encourage them to see themselves—as valid members of the community just the way they are.

The emerging concept of equal dignity has also affected relationships between men and women. There are clear signs that men's and women's traditional roles have outplayed themselves. True, men and women often think, experience, and act in very different ways. To what extent these differences are biological or cultural-historical in origin is not important in this context. The principle of equal dignity stresses that people are different, but it does not strive to equalize or resolve this difference. That is why this principle can be applied to personal relations between men and women, adults and children, Hindus and Christians, Africans and Scandinavians, doctors and patients, or employers and employees.

What do I mean by "equal dignity"? Whereas "equality" is a static, measurable entity, "equal dignity" refers to a dynamic intrepersonal process. It is not a quality that is established and remains in place. Instead it must constantly be adapted to new circumstances that arise.

Equal dignity also differs from equality in that it is not necessarily reflected in any particular allocation of roles. For example, the fact that a wife prepares food in the kitchen on a Sunday afternoon while her husband watches football on TV—or the other way around—does not tell us anything about the degree of equal dignity that exists between them. Even though this distribution of roles may appear very traditional, it does not imply that the roles are unequal—unless one partner feels coerced into assuming that role by the other. When a person assumes a new role, equality becomes relevant only if the person assuming these new responsibilities becomes more of a person as a result. In other words, when fathers devote more time to their children, their wives may feel grateful to have one less responsibility. But the partnership between parents only grows to the extent that fathers experience themselves as more complete human beings as a result of their contact with their children. Otherwise they are merely "helping out."

Our ability to behave spontaneously with equal dignity in relation to an adult partner or a child depends, like so many other things, on the experiences we had in the family in which we grew up and the role models we encountered. It can be difficult to meet other people with equal dignity if we didn't experience it as a child. It can be especially difficult for those who have been doted on because of their appearance, ability to cooperate, or success at school. For most people, the ability to treat others with equal dignity requires learning and daily training.

Children Cooperate!

When children cease to cooperate, it is either because they have cooperated too much for too long, or because their integrity has been harmed. It is never because they are uncooperative.

The Basic Conflict

From reading the earliest written documents, we know that the fundamental existential dilemma has always been the conflict between the individual and the group or society. Sometimes this is referred to as a conflict between individualization and conformity, or between identity and adaptation. I choose to call it the conflict between integrity and cooperation.

Fig. 1

INTEGRITY

Personal boundaries, needs, emotions, reactions, values, beliefs

CONFLICT

Static conflict leads to pain, signals, symptoms, syndromes

COOPERATION

copy/imitate, adapt, conform

All theories of how to bring up children have been based on a particular reading of this conflict: namely, that children are potentially uncooperative, asocial, or egocentric. Therefore, the task of adults has been to teach children how to cooperate, adapt them-selves, and take others into consideration. The means by which this task was accomplished have varied. In the second half of the past century, for example, the use of physical violence has declined, and the use of conversation has increased.

The belief that children were uncooperative went unchallenged until very recently. At the time of my birth, for example, pediatricians recommended structure and hygiene, a system that came to be known as "Quietness, Cleanliness, and Regularity." Mothers were informed that they had to breastfeed, bathe, and put their infants to bed at certain times and at regular intervals. If the parents failed in these objectives, these experts argued, children would assume control of their parents! When, after a few weeks or months, a mother grew worried that her child was often frustrated and cried, the experts had a ready answer: they warned her of the dangers of straying from the schedule while assuring her that crying was good for children—it exercised their lungs. Fortunately for many of us—at least those of us who survived the first years of our lives in relatively good shape—our parents didn't have the heart to listen to our cries of frustration for too long. They went against doctors' orders and picked us up and fed us when they weren't supposed to.

There's another assumption that went unchallenged until recently: given the conflict between children's need to keep their personal integrity intact and their desire to cooperate, most experts said that children would look out for themselves. Parents, therefore, had to help children learn to cooperate on adult terms, so that children would know from the start who was in charge.

After forty years of intensive research into families, and two decades of probing study into the early mother-child relationship, we have learned that the reality is quite the opposite. In fact, when children have to choose between preserving their own integrity and cooperating—and this happens to them, as it does to adults, scores of times every day—children choose cooperation nine times out of ten. Thus children do not need adults to teach them how to adapt or how to cooperate. What they do need, however, is adults who can teach them how to look after themselves when they are interacting with others.

Adults have difficulty seeing this problem for two reasons. First of all, we do not normally pay much attention to children's behavior when they cooperate; only when children stop or refuse to cooperate they way we want them to do we sit up and take notice. Secondly, children's cooperation can be mani-fested in two very different behaviors. But before getting into this distinction, let me define what I mean by cooperation.

Cooperation

When I say that children cooperate, I mean that they copy or imitate the most important adults around them—initially, their parents, and subsequently other adults with whom they have close contact.

Example: Mom's maternity leave has come to an end; it's time for six-month old Lily to begin attending day care. On the mornings that her mom takes Lily to day care before work, the child cries and is unhappy; nothing comforts her. When her dad takes Lily to day care, she seems fine.

It's a mystery! Why should this be? The parents have innumerable discussions about the quality of day care, and about their contrasting parenting styles: Is mom too protective? Is dad affectionate enough?

In the great majority of cases, however, the child's happiness or unhappiness upon arriving at day care has nothing to do with these factors. Rather, children like Lily cry with mom because, quite simply, the mother (for good reasons) is not emotionally ready to be separated from her child. She is anxious, sad, nervous, or unhappy—and has been since giving birth. But she has also suppressed these feelings because the family's situation is such that it is not possible for one of the parents to stay at home.

Even though the mother is no longer conscious of these feelings, Lily senses them—and copies them. The child, in other words, is cooperating by competently communicating a message that can be translated as "Dear Mother: Something is wrong between us— something is unclear. I am just letting you know that I know this, and assume that you will take the responsibility for solving the problem, so that we both can feel better."

But if we were to ask the mother whether the screaming child she has just left at day care is cooperating with her, she would most probably say no. This is because the mother's concept of cooperation has more to do with adaptation; that is, she assumes that a cooperative child would endure their mutual leave-taking without tears.

The same dynamic is in operation when children are brought to the dentist or the doctor, or placed in any new situation.

Example: Karen and Christian have just had their first child, Sarah, after many years of involuntary childlessness. Karen has taken a year's leave from her work to stay home with her infant daughter. Like most other new parents, Karen and Christian are extremely happy and at the same time uncertain about whether they can live up to the enormous responsibility of parenthood.

For many reasons, they never have the opportunity to talk with each other about their uncertainty. This means that Karen has to cope with the baby on a daily basis without having sorted through her feelings. When Christian comes home from work or when friends and family drop in, they either inquire about Sarah's well-being or declare how wonderful it must be for Karen to have so much time together with her child.

Gradually, Karen suppresses her uncertainty and grows very particular about Sarah's hygiene and diet: her daughter must have nice clothes, she must not have a sore bottom, and she must eat regularly and preferably in great quantity.

At the age of three months, Karen's daughter begins to vomit the breast milk. Karen becomes desperate but does not mention the problem to anyone until the child begins to lose weight. Finally, she pulls herself together and broaches the subject with her pediatrician. Because there is a slim possibility that the child has been born with a narrow cardia, a hospital examination is arranged. The examination shows no physical disorder, but the child continues to vomit. Breastfeeding, which had previously been an intimate and pleasing experience, has now become a nightmare for mother and daughter alike.

Although Karen doesn't realize it, her daughter is cooperating and is giving her mother very competent feedback. Her message can be interpreted any number of ways.

The first instance of vomiting could have meant:

"Thank you, Mom. Now I'm full!"

or:

"Mom, I would rather eat when I'm hungry and not when you feel like enjoying an intimate experience with me!"

or:

"Something is wrong between us, Mom. You have become so obsessed with being a good mother that you have completely forgotten that I also have needs. Don't you think it would be a good idea to have a talk with Dad?"

or:

"Listen, Mom. I just can't take the way you're treating me. It makes me sick!"

But Karen doesn't think of her daughter as cooperative—quite the contrary.

Several weeks pass. After yet another hospitalization, Karen and Christian decide to contact a family therapist. (Most therapists would draw one of three conclusions: that Karen is neurotic, that the parents' marriage is on the rocks, or that there is something wrong with the child.) When asked directly how she thought Sarah could cooperate, Karen answered, "If only she would start to eat normally and begin to gain weight, I'd be happy."

But that is not the way children cooperate. They go to the root of the matter. Without being conscious of it, they always put their finger on the conflict that is preventing the family from achieving genuine well-being.

Example: A family is enjoying a meal at a restaurant. When coffee is served, the children, ages four and seven, are given ice cream, which they quickly finish. Meanwhile, the parents become totally engaged in an important and intimate conversation.

The children sit listening for a while, but soon they invent a game. They start to walk, very quietly, in ever increasingly complicated patterns, between the vacant tables in the restaurant. On a couple of occasions, the parents call to them and the children stop playing, but they quickly become involved in their game again.

Suddenly the father calls to them angrily, in a low voice. When they obediently approach the table, he says, "Didn't you hear me?

If you can't behave yourselves, you won't eat out with us again. Oh, never mind, that's enough for this time. We're going home!"

The children are dumbfounded. Without a word, they leave the place with downcast eyes, their shoulders hunched up to their ears. They have been cooperating—completely, openly, and directly. Their behavior said, "Since our parents are wrapped up in each other, we'll find something to do so we won't disturb them."

Now let's fast-forward a few months, to an evening when one of the children says to her father, "Can we go out for a pizza tonight?"

"Well, maybe," her father says. "But you'll have to behave yourselves and not spoil it like you did last time!"

Once again, a parent has misread a child's spontaneous, loving, and considerate behavior as "uncooperative." Once again, a parent has confused cooperation with "good behavior." He has chosen to focus on obedience rather than on establishing a relationship based on equal dignity and trust.

If we look at children's behavior differently, we might see that children are experts at cooperating in all areas. Think of the four-year-old boy who already walks like his father, the six-year-old girl who eats just like her mother, or the nine-year-old boy who talks to his younger brother exactly as his father talks to him. When we as parents see our children imitating us in these ways, we rarely become indignant or confused. To the contrary—we feel flattered.

But when children copy or express feelings and attitudes that we would prefer to keep to ourselves, or of which we are not aware, we are likely to react much more negatively. Very small children actually study us in order to read our feelings before expressing themselves. Note, for example, what happens when you visit a family with a child between the ages of six months and two and a half years: the child studies his mother's or father's face intensely for several seconds after you walk into the room. If either parent is agitated, nervous, afraid, or if she simply doesn't feel like receiving visitors, the child will start to cry or turn her face away from the visitor. At this point, the parent will probably assume an obliging social smile and say to you, "Oh, it's you! Do come in!" But her child will not be assuaged.

Similarly, children are on the alert if their mother entertains a new admirer although she is not sure of her feelings about him; or if their father begins dating but would rather keep this a secret from his child.

As a family therapist, I find examples of this type of copying every day. Children, especially young children, become agitated and demand attention during family sessions until their parents and I have pinpointed the family's problem. Once the problem is identified and the parents have accepted responsibility for dealing with the problem, younger children often fall asleep; those who are slightly older either start to draw or grow bored and want to go home. Very valuable feedback for all adults involved!

Children even copy their parents when conflicts and problems arise. Their tendency to do so has often led to speculation about the biological roots of alcoholism, for example. My experience with family therapy indicates to me that a child of an alcoholic parent who grows up to be an alcoholic is cooperating with the selfdestructive parent to whom she was particularly attached – i.e. hers or his pattern of behavior.

As I mentioned earlier, children's cooperative behavior can be manifested in two different ways. A child who cooperates in a straightforward way imitates a parent's behavior. In families in which neither parent is terribly destructive, children tend to copy parents straightforwardly.

- Children who are treated with respect treat others with respect.

- Children who are cared for care for others.

- Children whose integrity is not violated don't violate the integrity of others.

A child who cooperates in an inverted way acts in a way that seems oppositional because he is turning his behavior inward. Yet he is motivated by a desire to cooperate.

It is also not uncommon that two children in the same family cooperate in different ways. This often surprises both parents and professionals alike, since the children have the same background and are brought up in the same way.

Example: A young mother in a Croatian refugee camp approaches the psychosocial team in the camp because her seven-year-old son is impossible, defiant, whining, and clinging—in other words, disobedient and uncooperative. She describes her twelve-year-old son as helpful, mature, and cooperative. The teachers at the school describe him as introverted, but clever and diligent.

The family has been subjected to colossal upheavals. The woman's husband had been killed at the Bosnian front six months earlier; the remainder of her family is dispersed in various refugee camps and asylum centers. The mother has chosen to cope with these losses in the same way that most parents do: spontaneously, out of consideration for the children, she keeps her great bereavement to herself, only crying now and then when she is alone. This loving and well-intentioned gesture, unfortunately, is very common, but it is just as unhealthy for the mother as it is for her children.

The elder son cooperates with his mother by doing what she does. Having lost the spark of life, he keeps his sorrow to himself. Hunched over, he walks around with a slightly mechanical gait and an inscrutable, stony look on his face. From the adults he meets he elicits sympathy and care. His unspoken feelings for his mother calm and fortify both of them. In my view, he cooperates with her in a straightforward way. He simply does what she does.

The younger brother also cooperates, but in an inverted way. He does the opposite. He is the only one in the family who actively expresses his sorrow, desperation, frustration, and longing for companionship. In other words, he tries to give voice to the feelings that his mother suppresses. But his mother cannot simultaneously inure herself to her own feelings and open herself to his: their feelings are too similar for this to be possible. He too would like to cooperate just as his big brother does, but he cannot bring himself to do so. His half-choked expressions of frustration do not evoke the sympathy of other adults, but rather evoke their own helplessness and irritability. He is not seen as "big and sensible" like his brother. He is seen as "little and naughty." All three cooperate at the expense of their health. But only the younger son holds the key to a healthier family. It is he who shows the way.

Fortunately, the mother is aware enough to realize that she needs help. She understands the danger signs and takes them seriously enough to talk to other adults about her problem. Eventually, she is introduced to a group of women in similar situations. As she comes to terms with her own grief, she enables her elder son to express his. As a consequence, the younger son calms down.

We often see the same phenomenon—divergent cooperative behavior—in families in which the father is violent toward both his wife and/or his children. Frequently, one child imitates dad, becoming outwardly violent and destructive, while the other, imitating mom, directs the violence inward. Children like this become either outwardly self-destructive— abusing drugs, becoming sexually promiscuous, or attempting suicide—or they become quiet and self-effacing, refuse to make personal commitments, and have an exaggerated sense of responsibility in relation to others. Note that on the surface many of these more subtle behaviors are often mistaken for signs of a "good upbringing."

By the time the children in such families become adolescents, they behave in radically different ways. For many reasons, boys still tend to become violent while girls tend to become self-destructive. One of the main reasons for this phenomenon is that girls often take their mother as a model and therefore cooperate with her self-destructive pattern of behavior. Upon closer examination, however, it may be that all children relate to their parents differently, both in the nature and the quality of their interactions.

Here's a schematic way to understand the issue of straightforward and inverted imitation/cooperation:

- Children who are criticized become either critical of others or self-critical.

- Children who are brought up in violent homes become either violent or self-destructive.

- Children who are brought up in nonexpressive families become either silent or talkative.

- Children who are subjected to violent or sexual abuse become either excessive and self-destructive or excessive and abusive.

In my estimation, fifty percent of children who are confronted with destructive behavior from adults cooperate in an inverted way. The other fifty percent cooperate straightforwardly and are identified as "problems" because of it. And destructive behavior is far from always brutal, autocratic or abusive. It can also be overly sweet, submissive and defensive. I mention this to underscore the fact that we all have our good reasons for doing what we do. We have all innocently been led to our destructive/ self-destructive behavior.

Many adults act in ways that they believe are loving and caring but that in fact are not. Others intend to act in loving ways, but intention alone is not sufficient. In days past, when the family was an autocratic power structure, parents could more easily suppress the competence of children. Luckily, doing so has become much more difficult. Not only have children and young people become more self-assured, but parents have also become more flexible and society as a whole is more inclined to take the wellbeing of the individual child seriously.

Integrity

When I use the word "integrity," I refer to a collective concept that relates to the wholeness and inviolability of our physical and psychological existence. To talk about integrity raises issues of identity, limits/boundaries, personal needs and values

In most cases, children cannot protect their integrity in relation to their parents. By this I don't mean to imply that they are wholly incompetent in this area: they can, in fact, set their own limits to a great extent. Rather, I mean that they often disregard their own needs if these needs conflict with their parents'; they choose to cooperate instead of thinking of themselves.

To illustrate this, consider incest. The sexual abuse of children or stepchildren by fathers or mothers is a dramatic violation of a child's physical, emotional and existential integrity. When incest victims describe how they felt during the attack, they often say that they knew what occurred was totally wrong, and that they tried, verbally and nonverbally, to defend themselves. Hearing these accounts, a loving adult can't imagine a scenario in which another adult could ignore the victim's pleas to stop the attack. All incest victims have abandoned their own limits in order to cooperate. And when threatened or otherwise manipulated, the incest victim will often even promise the perpetrator not to reveal what happened. Sometimes this loyal, cooperative silence lasts several years; in other cases it lasts a lifetime.

Clearly this is a self-destructive reaction to an injustice that society regards as not only illegal but morally objectionable on the highest order. It does not take much to imagine how silent and self-destructive children deal with everyday injustices of a lesser magnitude—those that are commonly accepted as a valuable or necessary part of a "good upbringing."

Generally, children react self-destructively toward violations. That is, when parents, consciously or unconsciously, violate their children's integrity in the same way and at regular intervals, children do not conclude that their parents have acted wrongly. They assume that they themselves are wrong! Losing their sense of self-esteem, they accumulate a sense of guilt or shame. Such an interchange has lifelong consequences, both for the children's quality of life and for the quality of the parent-child relationship.

It is a sad fact that the more a person's integrity is violated, the more he or she tends to cooperate with and submit to the violator. This is not only true for children but also for women who live with violent partners. Clinicians who work with adult torture victims have observed that there is a relationship between the degree of violation and the sense of guilt. The pronounced goal of torture is to destroy the integrity of the victim just short of having the victim die. From the point of view of the torturer, torture is most successful when the victim feels completely ashamed of what happened.

Similarly, children who have been institutionalized because of parental abuse—physical and psychological cruelty—suffer from an extreme lack of self-esteem and an enormous sense of guilt. They also evince a sense of loyalty toward their parents and often feel compelled to go home for weekends and holidays, knowing they may get seriously hurt.

Children whose integrity has been violated have always been competent in communicating this violation to adults, but their message has often been ignored, suppressed, or misinterpreted.

When I was a child, for instance, it was quite normal for parents and teachers to believe that you could make children "good" by telling them how "bad" they were. Children would only become "well behaved" if adults told them with sufficient conviction how badly behaved they were.

But to tell children that they are wrong is to violate their integrity, and they often communicate this violation nonverbally, in clear and unambiguous language: they cry or their faces assume a pained expression; they look at the adult for a moment and, if their message is not understood, their bodies become stiff, they lower their eyes toward the ground, and their faces drop toward their chests. Everything about them says, "You're hurting me!"

In fact, some children actually say, "You're hurting me!" only to be told, "Be quiet when I'm talking to you!" In other instances, adults misread children's body language as defiance and respond by saying, "Look at me when I'm talking to you!" Both rejoinders reinforce an external, social ideal at the expense of the child's personal integrity. Comments such as these say to the child, "It is not important if what I say hurts you or not—and if it does, perhaps you'll remember it better! What is more important is that you learn normal politeness, and that means looking at the person who's talking to you!"

If this exchange does not impress the child sufficiently, adults sometimes take hold of the child's chin and force it upward. In this case, there is only one line of defense left for the child: downcast eyes. But this reaction so infuriates some parents that they resort to physical violence or tell the child to go to her room until she changes her mind.

Why was this practice, so common in Denmark thirty or forty years ago, and still used in many countries, considered normal and acceptable? There are two reasons.

First, all parents did it, which made it seem correct by definition. Second, and most important in this context, children cooperate! The child who is beaten or sent to bed without dinner will come to her senses, two hours later, or perhaps the next morning, and resume her loving relationship with her parents. She will play ball with her father, talk intimately with her mother, and run around the yard with her friends. Perhaps she will ritually apologize to her parents, or perhaps her parents will take the initiative by saying, "Let's just forget about our fight, now that everything's fine."

The girl is not furious with her parents and does not regard them more critically than she did before. Yet she has lost another small amount of self-esteem—she has become a little less herself and a little more the way her parents want her to be. But just like all other children, she loves her parents completely unconditionally and is prepared to give them the daughter they want, almost irrespective of the price. So convinced is she that they are right and she is wrong that she will most probably repress the pain and the humiliation. In fact, twenty years later, she will probably do the same thing to her own child.

This ability of children to cooperate is often used to support the theory that one particular method of upbringing is the "right" one, or that children will not really be "harmed" by what we adults subject them to. Parents point to cooperative children and say, "Aha! See, I told you we were raising johnny right. Look at the way he cooperates!"

Example: A young mother had difficulty coping with all the household responsibilities awaiting her upon her return home from work. Separated from her children's father, she had to look after her three-year-old daughter and five-year-old son, clean, cook, do the laundry, and tend to the family finances all by herself. Her solution was to tell the children that they had to stay in their room and watch television for a few hours every day while she tended to her chores.

The children's teachers noticed that the children were somewhat passive and looked a little sad at school. When asked what was wrong, the boy complained about being forced to stay in his room. The teacher then called the mother, who not only openly admitted that she banished her children to their room but defended her decision in two ways: her own mother had done the same to her and no harm had come of it; in addition, she could hear the children playing when she walked by their room, and they sounded happy. Of course, the children weren't happy; they were merely cooperating.

I raise this example not to debate whether it's right or wrong to confine children to their rooms for a few hours a day. Rather, I wish to emphasize that children give us clear signals, and that we have to take them seriously— even if this flies in the face of how we ourselves were raised, or how others are raising their children.

Physical violence is an insult to any person's integrity—including children's. We may attempt to rationalize it by saying it's "the only solution," or by saying, "He had it coming to him," or by defending an adult's right to inflict corporal punishment. Indeed, the sheer number of euphemisms we have coined in order to blunt the impact of our behavior should tip us off that we are doing something we know is wrong.

In spite of this, many adults use the same kind of arguments to defend corporal punishment as the mother who confined her children to their room: "I had a few good hidings when I was a child—I deserved them, and they didn't do me any harm." And "It works! When children do something wrong, a good hard smack ensures that they won't do it again."

The argument that "it works" is cited not only by parents but also by educational and mental health professionals. On the surface, they're right. These methods do work. In fact, the more one party demands that the other sacrifice his or her integrity, the better the methods seem to work. This is why a six-year-old incest victim resembles a flirty thirteen-year-old Lolita, and why japanese schoolchildren commit suicide because of achievement anxiety. It's why new religious sects, each with its own gimmick, have so much appeal. It's why tens of thousands of people weep when a Stalin or a Tito dies. It's why patriarchal fathers and power-sick grandmothers can live under the illusion that they have their whole family behind them, when in fact they have the family *under* them.

But to defend corporal punishment by claiming its efficacy is mistaken for two reasons. First, we've seen that children willingly cooperate with any adult whom they love, trust, and depend on, no matter how the adult behaves. Second, now that we know so much about the long-term emotional, cognitive and spiritual effects of violence, it is simply unethical to justify the use of violence simply because it works in the short run.

In other words, it is no longer sufficient to claim that something "works." We must examine why and how it works. We have to start asking less primitive questions about how we treat each other. We need to consider the human and social price that we ourselves, and our children, clients, patients, and other members of society have to pay for what, on the surface, appears to be a successful means of achieving cooperation. If the price is the sacrifice of one's integrity, then the price is too high. That is a simple and civilized ethical principle.

In the past, when we still believed that children were born incompetent semi-humans, it was possible to justify violating their integrity. Adults who were in power had power to interpret and describe reality. Adults also knew, implicitly, what was best for children. They knew what was required for children to be able to grow up and become real people.

- "You'll realize the value of it when you grow up!"

- "It's for your own good!"

- "One day you'll thank me for this!"

- "It hurts me more than it hurts you!"

These are just some of the classic assertions that have been uttered as adults violated the integrity of children and young people. Interpreted in the most sympathetic light, these statements reveal both how uncomfortable the adults felt about acting as they did, and the social necessity that they act in this particular way.

Now we know better. Not only do we know that children are competent; we also know that they

- are social beings from birth;

- can express the content and limits of their integrity;

- cooperate competently with every kind of adult behavior, irrespective of whether it is healthy or destructive to them;

- competently express, both verbally and nonverbally, the nature of the emotional and existential dilemmas that their parents are experiencing.

In short, children are of most value to the lives of their parents at the time when they are generally thought of as most troublesome!

During the course of this book, I will attempt to illustrate and substantiate this perhaps somewhat provocative observation, which is one of the cornerstones for building a new type of relationship between parents and children. Here are just three examples.

Example:

When Nicolas is eleven months old, his parents experience a serious crisis in their marriage. Often they sit up arguing into the early hours of the morning.

Every time this happens, Nicolas wakes up and cries. His parents hold him in an attempt to cheer him up, but nothing seems to help. In spite of all their efforts, he is inconsolable. The more they try to discover what he needs, the more clinging and irritating he becomes—until, exhausted, he finally falls asleep about an hour later. The next morning, as a rule, he's mopey and irritable.

His parents, who are aware that children are competent, know that Nicolas is not behaving in this way to "command attention" or to disturb them. As they try to understand his behavior, they realize that these crying episodes remind them of a similar phenomenon: Nicolas also tends to wake up while they are making love—but at these times he is always happy and at ease, and it is not difficult to get him to fall asleep again. In this context, they readily acknowledge the destructive nature of their late-night fights. Not only does the tone of their conversation quickly become reproachful and unpleasant, but the arguments never really resolve anything. In the end, they simply feel tired, touchy, and disheartened.

After a period of weeks, the parents find more constructive ways to discuss their disagreements and differences. Nicolas still wakes up, a little frustrated and unhappy, but after five or ten minutes of sitting with them while they talk, he calms down and asks to be put back to bed.

By taking their son's reaction seriously, the parents learned a lesson that otherwise might have taken them years to discover. They realized that his distress and frustration meant: "Dear Mom and Dad, I don't like the way you're trying to solve your problems. It makes me afraid and unhappy. Couldn't you find another way of doing it?" After they changed the way they disagreed, Nicolas changed his message: "I still get a bit afraid and unhappy when you two disagree, but I'm reassured about the way you're tackling things!"

Example: Louise is a difficult, demanding nine-year-old who begins to behave in an alarmingly self-destructive manner: she cuts her fingers with scissors, pricks the skin of her stomach with a knife, and pushes a needle up her nose to cause nosebleeds. She has an older brother to whom she often compares herself. For several years she has been saying to her parents, "Why don't you love me as much as you love Thomas?" Her provocative, self-inflicted nosebleeds began shortly after Thomas had been to the doctor to have the veinlets in his nose cauterized because he often suffered from serious, unprovoked nosebleeds.

Louise's parents are competent adults who love their daughter very much, and they have tried everything that was in their power to improve their relationship with her. They are sensible and reasonable; they try to give her all that she demands. Other adults with whom they have discussed their daughter recommend that they set consistent limits. But Louise persists in her troubling behavior. On a few occasions, she literally asks her parents to attend a "meeting" at which she says, "It can't go on like this, the way we treat each other. Shouldn't we try to be good friends from now on?"

The problems continue. Both parents feel defensive, exhausted, and perplexed. They are not angry or irritated with their daughter and do not demand to have her "examined and repaired." But when Louise begins to harm herself, their feelings turn to guilty unhappiness and they realize that they need help.

When the family entered therapy, we began to examine the relationship between Louise and her parents from her birth, and certain factors became clear:

- Her mother had had a problematic pregnancy, and the birth had been painful and complicated.

- Louise had been difficult from the start—restless, noisy, and a problematic eater. Her mother felt incompetent and on the defensive.

- Louise's mother had experienced problems with her milk supply when breast-feeding, and the other mothers in the maternity ward had looked at her and Louise reproachfully.

- Louise's father had been extremely involved in his work, as he was in the throes of starting his own business. According to his own account, a couple of years had passed before he had really become involved with his daughter and realized that his wife had had difficulties in establishing a harmonious relationship with Louise.

From the time she was born, Louise lacked the fundamental sense of security that children need if they are to develop in a healthy way. In particular, she did not have the sense that she was in secure, competent hands. Her mother felt that she was on the defensive most of the time, and that she was left to find a solution to her difficulties by herself.

In this situation, the infant Louise was faced with two possibilities: she could resign herself and become a so-called "easy" child, or she could actively struggle in order to obtain what she lacked. Louise "chose" the latter.

Some child development researchers have become convinced in recent years that children are born with a particular "character." But from my vantage point it is not particularly important whether Louise's strong-willed and challenging nature was a result of her genetic makeup or if it was a more unique psychological expression of her way of cooperating. What is important, however, is the way in which parents recognize the difference between their children's characters and vitality. This determines whether a child's character turns constructive or self-destructive.

Louise, for example, cooperated with her mother by acting in a way that said, "Dear Mother, you seem to be somewhat perplexed and uncertain as to how you should look after me, so I'll have to make myself very clear. I'll make sure that I protest when you do something

I don't like, and that I demand things when there is something I want!"

When she did speak aloud, she tried to address her dilemma by saying: "Why don't you love me as much as you love Thomas?" Traditional psychology (and ordinary plain common sense) would interpret this question as an expression of jealousy—but I don't. What Louise is saying is that she is not being loved in the right way. This makes her feel as if she is not of value to her parents— and being of value to one's parents is something to which we all desperately aspire when we are children.

When children (or adults) don't feel of value, they become irritable, aggressive, and frustrated. To cope with these complicated feelings is beyond the capacity and maturity of just about any child. Imagine four-year-old Louise saying to her parents, "Look here! Something is wrong between us. I know that you love me, and I do everything within my power to deserve your love. But most of the time, I still feel unloved. When I look at your relationship with my big brother, I can see that you get along much more easily with him than with me, and I find it very difficult not to be envious." Exactly! That's not the way children talk although it's what they wish to convey.

But when parents and professionals misinterpret Louise's experience and mislabel her feelings as "jealousy," Louise feels as if she is in the wrong, which in turn leads her to intensify her "jealous" behavior. This vicious circle happens with adults as well.

Louise's parents reacted as the majority of loving parents would. To her protestation that they loved her brother more, they replied, "But, Louise, that's not true! We love you just as much as we love Thomas!" This answer is both honest and true, and it is meant lovingly, but it has precisely the opposite effect: Louise experiences herself as being even more alone and more wrong. Louise might say to herself, "I can see they love me, and I can hear that they love me. But since I can't feel that they love me, there must be something wrong with me."

Now let's return to Louise's initial way of cooperating—her demandingness. She needs constant attention. Often, she asks for the impossible—a particular kind of icecream cone in the middle of the winter, for example. Every night in bed, without fail, she calls for her parents to come to her room ten to fifteen times. Their time together is consumed by the dramas that ensue when her parents are either unable or unwilling to meet the child's requirements. Louise does not just allow herself to be rejected!

This kind of behavior is also often misinterpreted. Parents of children like Louise are urged to "set limits," "stand firm," "say no," "be consistent," and so forth. The problem is that these childrearing methods only touch the surface of the problem—just as interpreting the child's plea for love as jealousy is a superficial explanation. The real problem is that children do not know what they need. Often they only know what they want. This does not mean that children are incompetent in the area of getting their needs met. It means that they lack the necessary perspective and linguistic ability to express themselves. Indeed, they hope and count on their parents to express what they cannot.

But, even though children can't express what they need, they know perfectly well when their needs are not being met, and they are capable of giving adults competent feedback—sometimes by acting frustrated ("difficult") or by becoming totally resigned and passive.

Active, vigorous children like Louise impulsively demand everything they want. Irrespective of how much they receive back, their demands escalate, becoming more numerous and absurd. Naturally, adults find this behavior immensely provocative. In those cultures that still esteem the "old-fashioned" child-rearing principles, this kind of behavior can be suppressed with the use of physical violence and/ or verbal assault. Most likely, the child's irrational behavior will disappear, only to find expression when she becomes an adult.

Some families strive for a more considerate and democratic form of upbringing. Unfortunately, over the course of the last ten to fifteen years, we have seen an increasing number of these families tyrannized by children who are apparently completely self-centered and asocial. This tends to happen when parents are afraid of being authoritarian and are unsure of how to bring their personal authority and sense of limits to the negotiation. As a result, these parents often end up "servicing" their children. In turn, the children get too much of what they want and too little of what they need. Furthermore, when parents relate to their children by providing "service," both parties become lonely. (Some children have always received too little of what they need; what has changed, thanks to more liberal child-rearing attitudes and greater economic prosperity, is that there are more children who get too much of what they want. This phenomenon is particularly noticeable in some of the recently democratized Eastern European countries in which a relatively small group of people has suddenly become wealthy. Naturally parents in these families bestow some of this wealth on their children, often in the form of material possessions that confer social status.)

Louise used three approaches to inform her parents that she did not feel of value to them. First, she became increasingly demanding, and then she began verbalizing her feelings. Neither approach worked. Both she and her parents exhausted their energy, creativity, and mutual love in what seemed like a futile attempt to create a more harmonious relationship. But their efforts were not fruitless. The fact that Louise had fought so energetically and that her parents had been equally energetic in attempting to solve the problem bodes well for the child's future growth and development. Her prognosis would have been much more dire if she and her parents had simply given up on each other.

Inflicting pain on herself was Louise's third and final attempt to get her parents' attention. Her actions said, "It's painful for me to be with you . . . I'm bleeding!" This time, her parents listened.

During my conversations with this family, I learned that Louise's mother had been physically violated by her father all through her childhood. She had cooperated by becoming the sweet and obedient girl who always fulfilled the needs of others; as a result she had never discovered her own needs nor learned to express them. Thus she and Louise now had to go through the same learning process—together! At a relatively late age, the mother was forced to learn how to feel and express her own needs and limits so that her daughter could learn the same. Ironically, it was Louise who gave her mother the courage to come to terms with the abuse she had been subjected to as a child. In this light, Louise's behavior was valuable—on a deep, existential level—for her mother's life and for her parents' life together. This revelation would never have happened if Louise's demanding behavior had been defined as a "problem of upbringing." Under the most fortunate circumstances, a more superficial pedagogical strategy might have helped Louise become easier to live with. Her parents would have felt more confident. But Louise's compliance would have been bought at a very steep price—the irretrievable loss of the child's self-esteem.

Now let's consider another example of children's ability to give accurate emotional feedback.

Example:

A well-dressed, confident Italian family on vacation entered a restaurant for dinner. The parents and two girls, ages four and ten, emitted an aura of elegance. According to the menu, which the headwaiter presented to them, each guest had the choice of three appetizers, three main courses, and so forth. The father made his choice, the mother made hers, the older daughter ordered what her mother had, and the mother chose for the younger—who protested the order in a quiet but firm voice, making clear what she would have preferred. The father sat with a menacing glint in his eyes, and the mother cut the younger child short by saying, "You don't like that anyway!" And so the order stood. The older girl sat through the entire intermezzo, which lasted less than a minute, looking down at her plate.

When the first course arrived, the mother took the younger daughter's portion and cut it into small mouthfuls. Without a word of protest, the girl refused to eat. Both parents tried to persuade the girl to eat but to no avail. As the dishes were cleared in preparation for the arrival of the main course, the younger daughter was warned that she had better behave decently—or else. Among other threats, the girl was told that she would not be allowed to help herself to the lavish dessert buffet if she persisted.

At the arrival of the main course, the mother again cut the little girl's food into small pieces and pushed a forkful into her mouth. The girl ate the whole portion slowly and reluctantly and, when the parents presented her with her promised reward—the free choice of dessert—she announced that she did not feel like any. The other members of the family glanced knowingly at each other and shook their heads over the girl's "childish stupidity."

The following evening, the drama repeated itself, only this time the young girl refused to eat any of her food. After the main course, the father ordered his wife to put the girl to bed as a punishment for her embarrassing behavior. (The girl was as calm and silent as she had been on the first night. What embarrassed her parents was that the waiter might discover the uneaten food and remove it.)

On the third evening, the family received "therapy" from an unlikely source: the headwaiter. After taking the parents' and the older daughter's orders (she always ordered precisely the same food as her mother and always received the same discreet nod of acknowledgment from her parents), he turned toward the younger girl and asked, "And what would the young lady like to eat this evening?"

The girl looked up at him, surprised and happy. Abruptly, her posture changed. On previous evenings, she had sat on the chair correctly (but uncomfortably). Now she knelt so that she could assume the same height as the rest of the family. Then she said, "Could you tell me the choices again?"

"Of course, miss," replied the headwaiter, explaining the menu with the same attention to detail that he had lavished on the others. Skillfully, the girl placed her order, and before her somewhat dumbfounded parents had recovered their powers of speech, she began to converse with them as if nothing unusual had happened. Needless to say, the girl ate her food down to the last bite.

This scene repeated itself over the next few days with one important change—on each succeeding night, the atmosphere at the table became more convivial and natural. The father even permitted himself to come to the table in a casual shirt without a tie. Good upbringing had suffered a decisive, if not definitive, defeat. Led by a competent four-year-old (abetted by a wise waiter), the emotional life of this family had been liberated. The girl had won the battle that most children lose without a fight: the right to decide for herself what she wanted to put into her mouth, when, and in what quantity. She insisted on preserving her own integrity. Her parents observed her competence, accepted it, and allowed their lives to be enriched by it. And although the girl's older sister didn't realize it at the time, she too would benefit: now that the family was more accommodating, there was every reason to think that her upcoming adolescence would prove less problematic than it would have if her sister hadn't ordered her own food.

But what about the many children who are not lucky enough to have flexible parents or to meet an ingenious headwaiter? What can be done about those parents and other adults who become paralyzed at the first sign of pain?

My experience is that there are many parents who are prepared to listen and learn—more than we think. But they need to be approached not with criticism and accusation but with empathy and understanding. It's true that these parents often treat their own children critically—but that is because they have suffered the same pain that they are now inflicting, and they have suffered longer than their children have. We need to be able to see their own competence, just as they need to see the competence in their own children. We need to approach them as we wish them to approach their children.

The Conflict Between Integrity and Cooperation

When adults and children interact, behavior that we consider moral may in fact be unethical.

Adults and children experience dozens of situations every day during which we are faced with a seemingly "either/or" choice: should we be true to ourselves (that is, value our own integrity, our own personal limits and needs) or should we compromise what we want for the sake of maintaining relationships (that is, give in to external demands out of fear of retribution or rejection, or out of a desire to adhere to social norms)? (Whether this conflict can be restructured so that the answer is "both/and" depends on family and cultural traditions concerning dialogue and negotiation and is intimately connected with the individual's ability to express him-or herself personally. I will explore this idea later in the book.)

In the conflict between integrity and cooperation, children usually choose to cooperate, thereby disregarding themselves, particularly if they are subjected to even the most subtle pressure from parents. To comprehend the scope of this tendency, it is essential to realize that we are not just talking about the (more or less) premeditated pressure that parents put on their children, such as the way we choose to raise our children, the institutions to which we send them, where we choose to live, and how we choose to work. Clearly, these decisions exert pressures on children that are of great importance. But these conscious, premeditated choices are only a small part of the picture.

The greater part of the forces that influence our children is made up of the many phenomena and processes that we are less conscious of, and therefore have very little or no control over (at least not during the years when most of us are raising young children): the ups and downs in our marriage, our existential inner conflicts, our differing temperaments and degree of emotional openness, deaths in our immediate family, pressures at work, economic crises or civil war, and so on.

For example, an important component of children's physical integrity is their right to consume food when they are in need of it and not to consume food when they do not require it. Yet this basic right is frequently tampered with.

Example:

Most days, five-month-old Sarah dutifully eats a whole portion of mashed vegetables for lunch. One day, after she has eaten four spoonfuls, she refuses to open her mouth for the fifth. Her mother reacts initially by "soft-soaping" her, and when that does not help, she starts playing the old game: "Look, Sarah, Brmmmmm . . . brmmmmm . . . brmmmmm . . . Look, here comes a little airplane . . . right to your mouth." After a couple of attempts, Sarah starts to wail. Her mother strokes her hair, says some words of comfort, and then tries the airplane again. Sarah gives in and swallows everything that is pushed into her mouth.

Sarah's mother is caught up in a common obsession among new parents: that a child's healthy appetite is demonstrable proof of good parenting. She pressures her daughter in a conscious, premeditated way.

Example: Laura, also five months old, is supposed to be nursing, but she's not taking any milk even though her mother tries switching breasts and enticing the child with words. Suddenly irritable, the mother lifts Laura up, holds her out in front of her, and shakes her, saying, "Now, that's enough of that! I haven't got time to sit here all day while you decide what you want. Eat and that's that!" Laura drinks a few mouthfuls and falls asleep.

Laura's mother was a troubled, unemployed, young single parent who had had little education. Her daughter was literally the only thing that gave her life meaning. Often she could not distinguish between her own needs for closeness and intimacy and Laura's needs. As a result, she often kept Laura awake when she needed to sleep, and fed Laura when she wasn't hungry. She's pressuring her daughter in an unpremeditated way.

Both of these women want to care for their children, to make sure they have enough to eat. Yet both make a fundamental mistake—they ignore their child's signals. As parents, we must take responsibility for detecting both our premeditated and our unpremeditated mistakes. By this I mean that we must be vigilant as to the signals and symptoms that our children develop.

There is no such thing as a perfect family or a perfect society. The conflict between integrity and cooperation, if ongoing or un-resolved, will eventually produce signals or symptoms in all of us. The quality of family life is decided by the way adults deal with signals and symptoms in all members of the family, and their readiness to include individual pain in their conversation.

The more often we sacrifice our integrity for the sake of cooperation, the more pain we incur. We can become so good at repressing the pain that neither we ourselves nor those around us notice it. Inevitably, however, we emit a verbal or nonverbal signal indicating that something is wrong. If we and those closest to us take the signal seriously, understand its significance, and change the way we react, the conflict is solved and the pain eases or ceases. If none of these things happens, the signal increases or changes (becomes a physical act instead of a statement). Eventually, an actual symptom will reveal itself. The first signal is fatigue; the ultimate ones are murder or suicide.

Strictly speaking, there is nothing strange about this system of psychic functioning. Our body works in exactly the same way. Every cell has its own limits and identity and exists in a unique harmonious balance with other cells. When we violate the integrity of a cell—through the use of tobacco or other abusive substances— the body is thrown into a state of imbalance. If the violation persists, we become ill or experience pain. It's possible to recover from minor, time-limited violations, but the longer they continue, the more permanent harm we risk incurring.

When it comes to psychic violations, however, there is a great discrepancy between what our culture defines as a violation and what actually constitutes a violation. This is particularly true not only in relations between adults and children but also in those between men and women. There are many more real violations than we readily admit.

The integrity of children can be violated in three ways:

- The use of excessive physical violence, sexual abuse, or negligence, none of which society condones;

- The imposition of "good" or "necessary" child-rearing practices, most of which society approves of;

- The imposition of ideological positions, such as forced political or religious indoctrination.

This book defines violations of the integrity of the individual as unethical, which leads us to describe the discrepancy in what is considered a violation in another way: **in the interaction between adults and children, what is commonly accepted as good morality may quite possibly be bad ethics!** I do not mention this in order to point a moral or ethical finger at anyone, but simply to encourage adults to take a critical look at "what everyone does"—at what passes for "ordinary," "common," and "normal" in their culture.

According to my experience, it is particularly important that children and young people develop signals that can inform the adults who are responsible for them that the balance between integrity and cooperation has become distorted, and that they are in pain. As I will explain later, both parents and other adults can play an important, preventive role by actively helping children to learn to safeguard their own integrity.

But no adult is perfect and every child is different. Therefore we make "mistakes." Innocently, lovingly, and with the best intentions, we all make blunders. This is acceptable! What adults need to do is accept responsibility for their mistakes instead of blaming children, as they so often do. **In fact, adults often resort to an embarrassingly obvious double standard when describing their relationship with their children: if the relationship is successful, it's because the parents are good parents; if the relationship is unsuccessful, it's because the child is bad!**

Because we now recognize that children cooperate, we can venture two other conclusions about those children and young people whom we traditionally label "maladjusted" or "asocial":

- When a child behaves destructively and/or asocially, it is always because he is imitating, or cooperating with, one or more adults. Often the adult behavior is deemed "acceptable." But the adult violation always precedes the child's. Sometimes the adult acts this way to teach the child a "lesson," but often the adult behavior is motivated by self-destructive impulses.

- When a child ceases or refuses to cooperate, it is either because she has cooperated too much and for too long with destructive phenomena in her family, or because her integrity is being directly violated.

The list of signals manifested by children and young people is almost inexhaustible. Here are just a few of the classic comments parents make about their children in times of conflict:

- "He simply will not listen to what we say!"

- "She never comes home at the time we have agreed on!"

- "He's never hungry when the rest of us eat, but half an hour later he wants to eat."

- "All I do is clean up after them!"

- "It's a continual fight to get him to clean his room!"

- "The worst thing is that she also lies to us!"

- "He almost has to be driven to do his homework every day!"

- "If we don't wake her, she would never get up in the morning!"

- "You always have to ask them to do things. They never do anything without being asked!"

- "It's a job to get her dressed in the morning—that's how difficult she is!"

Phrased this way, these comments leave no doubt as to who is right and who is wrong. Educators, psychologists, and other professionals have traditionally either viewed the conflict through the lens of the parents, as expressed above, or blamed the parents as the problem.

Let's consider a couple of these conflicts individually. As I mentioned earlier, each family is unique, and it's impossible to interpret any behavior without intimate knowledge of the family in question. Therefore, the illustrations that follow are compiled from my general experience working with families.

"He simply will not listen to what we say!"

When children "simply won't listen," it's usually because what the parents are saying isn't worth listening to! Don't misunderstand: the parents may well be saying something that is true, sensible, reasonable, fair, or even ingenious. But they may express these noble sentiments in ways that are wrong, or in the wrong context, or in a way that goes against most people's personal values. It's possible, for example, that a child will cooperate with behavior that is extremely self-destructive without complaint, and then react against this behavior at another time when his lack of cooperation would be better tolerated. For most young children this is not a conscious choice. It's where their intuition and disposition take them.

It may also be true that the values underlying the parents' comment need to be revised. There are still many parents who believe that children must "learn to obey," despite the fact that this expectation nearly always results in "disobedience," whether overt or concealed. That's because we find it undignified and insulting to have to obey orders when we are more than willing to cooperate.

The motivation behind the child's reaction is easy to understand if we think about it in relation to our spouse or employer. "He only needed to ask me nicely," we say in an attempt to salvage our self-esteem after our boss has humiliated us. No one feels comfortable taking orders, not even those in the armed forces. Yet in that context, in which the goal is to train people to behave destructively, submission is required. The goal of a family is the opposite.

"He's never hungry when the rest of us eat, but half an hour later . . ."

Those children who don't want to eat with the family may simply have an idiosyncratic biological clock. But they may also be broadcasting an important signal: "I lose my appetite when I sit down to eat with the rest of the family. The atmosphere at the table is tense and destructive, and because I can't quite put it into words, I choose not to eat."

The shared daily meal (in the countries where this tradition still exists) is often the only time of the day when the entire family gathers together. Naturally, everyone will be sensitive at these times to the prevailing emotional atmosphere and will be reminded of unresolved conflicts. Many of us can remember how we as children felt in this situation. We are also reminded of it each time we sit down to a meal with friends or acquaintances whose ongoing yet concealed argument manages to leak out during the conversation.

One thing is certain: children do not engage in this kind of behavior to make life difficult for their parents. It is something they do for their family, not against it.

There are three other types of signals I want to consider:

- Psychosomatic symptoms: headache, stomachache, backache, muscular tension in the neck and shoulders, loss of weight or considerable weight gain, and so forth.

- Destructive behavior outside the home: behavioral problems ("bad behavior") at school; aggressiveness toward other children; hyperactivity; difficulties in concentrating; ganging up on others or being ganged up on; truancy; crime; abuse of alcohol, drugs, inhalants, prescription drugs, and so forth.

- Attempted suicide, silence and isolation, violence

Psychosomatic Symptoms

When we refer to "psychosomatic" signals and symptoms, we mean that the signal is physical (somatic) but has a predominantly psychological background. Medical science originally focused on the body alone and was somewhat slow to recognize soul and mind, the other two elements. All three constantly influence each other in ways and for reasons about which we know very little.

Generally speaking, people assume more personal responsibility for those problems that are psychosomatic rather than somatic in origin, reacting to them with a broad spectrum of behaviors ranging from acute embarrassment to anxiety about their own sanity. When children are described as having psychosomatic symptoms, parents often experience this diagnosis as an accusation. This is a pity because it prevents parents from trying to understand what is going on in their child's life.

No matter how resolved we are to look after our children, we can't ensure that their lives will be easy. We can love our children and prepare them to meet life as best we can, but we cannot protect them from the realities of existence. Pain is a natural part of every human life, from conception to death, and this includes the pain resulting from unresolved conflicts between integrity and coop-eration.

When children experiencing this conflict develop psychosomatic symptoms or signals, what they are saying is, "My life hurts right now, and I haven't yet found a constructive way of tackling it. And I don't know how to talk to anyone about it, because I can't find the words that express this pain. I am stuck in a conflict that I can't solve."

It is with psychosomatic symptoms as with symptoms manifesting in social behavior that they are best regarded as an "invitation":

"Hello out there! I'm not feeling well at the moment. Could somebody please come and visit me in my world and help me figure out what is wrong?"

Thankfully, we now understand that when children receive unsuitable psychological nourishment from their families, they often develop weight problems: for example, some eat too much, and others eat too little. We also know that a child bearing too much responsibility may develop muscular tension and headaches, and that stomachaches often develop in children who are experiencing anxiety or other deadlocked emotional conflicts.

My advice to parents whose child has developed a psychosomatic symptom is simple: look and learn. Try to see your child's life through his or her own eyes. It's more important to use this circumstance as an opportunity to get to know your child in a new way than it is to try to find the "cause." (It does not help to cross-examine a child. If a child knew what was wrong and had the right words to express it, the signal would be superfluous.) Gradually, you will discover how your child reacts psychosomatically when life becomes complicated. Some children develop an inflammation of the middle ear as infants and then have earaches many years later when they are under stress. Some get diarrhea or constipation. Some develop a cold and runny nose and others get a sore throat. Some children sleep all the time and others become physically hyperactive.

But some children develop psychosomatic symptoms and signals because they feel that it is impossible to talk to their parents about their distress. Sometimes this happens because psychosomatic symptoms are the "language" a particular family uses to "talk" about the pain, and to receive any attention one must learn to speak this language. Or it can be owing to the fact that the parents have so many arguments stemming from interpersonal difficulties that the children do not want to "disturb" them with their problems. It could also be because the parents simply do not listen when the children attempt to express themselves. The list of possible explanations could go on and on. The important point is this: psychosomatic signals and symptoms are coded signals. Adults have to take these signals seriously and help children to translate these signals into direct and clear language.

Destructive and Self-Destructive Behavior

When children become destructive, it is because one or more of the adults surrounding them violates their integrity verbally or physically or both. In some way, being with their parents (or caretakers) causes the children to lose self-esteem at a time in their lives when what they really need is to gain it.

The same dynamic applies to those children who become self-destructive, whether directly, through suicide attempts, or indirectly and gradually, through substance abuse or unsafe sexual practices. As I mentioned earlier, destructive and self-destructive behaviors are simply two different forms of cooperation in response to "accepted violations." In fact, it is common for children and young people to consciously accept the violations that are a part of family life. Children cooperate! It is the task of the adults to realize what the children are cooperating with.

Example: A nine-year-old boy arrived at school one morning with severe swelling on one side of his face. He had obviously been hit very hard. His mother was called to the school, and she admitted that she had hit him. She justified her action by saying that the boy had hit his three-year-old sister. "He mustn't do that kind of thing," she said. "It's wrong to hit those who are smaller than you are!" She had been hitting him for several years because she felt powerless in those situations in which she thought that he had not behaved properly.

As it turned out, this mother was alone with her three children most of the time; her husband worked on an oil rig and was away from home for long periods. Because she had difficulty coping with her role as a de facto single parent, she had recently started relying on the boy to look after the two younger children. Given the role of substitute father, he naturally copied his mother's definition of what it meant to be an "adult."

It is easy to criticize this mother for being hypocritical—punishing her son for hitting his sister by hitting him herself—but this is not the point. Once we examine her moral concepts, we realize that according to her beliefs, children must not hit smaller children, but adults are allowed to hit children if there is a good reason. She is simply one of the many adults who has learned, from her own upbringing in her particular culture, that children are not real people from birth, but that they can become people—by being beaten, if necessary.

Example:

Other situations are more difficult to understand. Three-and-a-half-year-old Peter, for instance, had become a problem at nursery school: he was biting his playmates when he became frustrated or could not get his own way.

Peter's parents were both interested and willing participants during three meetings that were subsequently arranged with a family therapist. From the beginning, they placed their cards openly on the table and admitted, among other things, that on a couple of occasions they had both given Peter a spanking when they did not know what else to do. But these incidents had occurred some time ago. Since the relationship between Peter and his parents was, in general, peaceful and pleasant, the family therapist doubted whether two or three spankings could have caused the current problem at school.

Peter was present at the meetings, which took place over the course of one month. During this time his relationships with the other children became less destructive, although he still bit them on occasion. Yet the adults at the meetings could not reach any conclusions about the real reason that Peter was biting the other children.

After a few months, Peter started biting again to such an extent that the adults became concerned and a new meeting was arranged. This time, Peter was difficult from the moment it began: he asked when they were going home, asked if he could draw but refused to use "those stupid pencils," wanted to sit on his parents' laps but only if they promised not to talk, and so forth.

Peter's father tried to get Peter to cooperate. He spoke to the boy quietly at first and appeared flexible, but inevitably he ended up raising his voice and saying things like, "Now that's enough!" "Now stop it!" "Now listen to me, Peter!" When the family therapist pointed out this phenomenon, the father answered quite spontaneously and with a very guilty look on his face, "Yes, you're probably right. My wife tells me that I'm always biting his head off!"

Everyone laughed—including Peter—now that the reason for Peter's behavior at nursery school had been revealed. The father explained that his own upbringing had been characterized by "no-nonsense methods," and when he became frustrated, he reverted to the same methods his father had used with him. The nursery school teacher who knew Peter best added that this was precisely what happened with Peter. If the child wanted a toy or a particular place at the table, he asked for it diplomatically—but when that method failed, he bit. Asked why she had not mentioned her husband's behavior at the earlier meetings, Peter's mother replied, "Because he doesn't do it as much as he did years ago, and I didn't want to criticize him when he had already changed so much."

Peter's mother then suggested that instead of "biting" at Peter when he was frustrated with his son, her husband could say, "Now I don't know what to say. I'll have to stop and think." This proved a good strategy for two reasons. Not only did the father find satisfactory solutions when he stopped to think, but Peter also changed the way he tackled his problems. Instead of biting other children, he retreated to a corner and sulked until he found something else to do. As the father's powers of negotiation grow, so will Peter's.

Often when I meet families such as Peter's it frightens me to think that for many years adults have characterized children like Peter as having "social problems," or "problems with relating to other children." It's not that these descriptions are wrong, but they are terribly superficial. Peter's inability to relate to other children was not his real problem but simply the smoke signal he sent up in order to call attention to his pain.

For generations now we have reacted to children's signals by instructing them about how they "should behave." As a result, the most cooperative of them have borne their pain without flinching. Even worse, they have hidden it so that it continues to distort their lives and gives them a false picture of themselves. The less cooperative have defied our instructions and escalated their "asocial" behavior until the adults surrounding them couldn't help but notice that something was wrong.

But a signal like Peter's *is* social in the most substantial and precise meaning of the word. What can be more social than informing those closest to him that being together with them caused him pain and that adjustments needed to be made for everyone's benefit? Ironically enough, many adults often tell children, "You have to think of everyone, not just yourself! You understand that, don't you?"

Tragically, but logically enough, we have done the same thing with those children whose signals evoke our sympathy and understanding as with those that arouse our anxiety and anger. Consider, for example, children who are extremely overweight. We feel for them when we see how mercilessly they are humiliated by their peers, and we implement physical training programs, nutritional treatment, and cooking classes so that they can lose weight and avoid being teased. This strategy is wellmeant but superficial—not only that, but it helps only a small minority of children. For those children and young people who are not capable of losing weight, our pedagogical efforts only add insult to injury. These methods make children feel as if something is wrong with them. They are another form of the teasing and humiliation they have to endure from their contemporaries.

A thirteen-year-old girl I know said it most clearly. Her parents had sought advice because they were concerned about her weight, which had increased dramatically in the space of a year. After several minutes of therapy, during which her parents had expressed their concern, Alecia stood up, threw out her arms and, with tears of anger rolling down her cheeks, shouted, "For Christ's sake, the only thing you can see is my flesh!"

Of course, this girl was exceptional because she had words for her existential dilemma. Most children cannot express themselves in this way. Unable to find the appropriate words for their pain, children (as well as many adults) tend to go along with the explanations, diagnoses, or stereotypes offered by others.

To sum up, physical survival in the past, whether under feudalism or dictatorship, often depended on one's ability to sacrifice one's integrity in order to cooperate with those in power. Parents who raised children to think this way were in fact giving them necessary life lessons—preparing them for adult citizenship. But this is no longer necessary. Most of the world now agrees that a society based on the abuse of power is below human dignity.

But even though the realities of society have so greatly changed in the course of the twentieth century, our basic assumptions regarding children's upbringing have remained the same. We generally believe that there is an inevitable clash of interest between the individual's need to maintain and develop integrity and society's needs for organization and development.

Based on my experience working with families and other kinds of groups, this basic assumption no longer is true. There is much to suggest that the opposite is the case: care for the integrity of the individual is a prerequisite if feelings for others are to develop in a healthy way. There is no collective growth unless it is based on individual growth.

Our new knowledge about the psychological development of children (and thereby humans) enables us to formulate new values to guide interaction between children and adults. These values need to be incorporated not only within the family but also in other contexts— day-care centers, schools, community centers— in which children and adults come together.

I propose a new paradigm: **Children's behavior, whether cooperative or disruptive, is just as important for the development and health of parents as the behavior of parents is for the development and health of children. The interaction between adults and children is a mutual learning process. The more we treat each other with equal dignity, the more we each gain.**

Self-Esteem
and Self-Confidence

Self-esteem, self-value, and self-confidence are often used synonymously. Although they are connected, they do not mean the same thing. In my view, it's very important that we understand their differences.

For the past fifty years, parents and educators—particularly those who work with children with so-called psychological and social problems—have been very aware of children's self-confidence and make great efforts to strengthen it.

But often their efforts are misguided for several reasons. Most significantly, they tend to address the wrong issue. They focus on strengthening children's self-confidence when the real problem is the children's lack of self-esteem. In addition, their efforts often backfire, leaving children with an even lower sense of self-esteem. And even when their attempts are successful, the success may be short-lived: the child's low self-esteem reemerges later on, often during times of stress, such as when the child encounters a dramatic and potentially self-destructive situation. The same dynamic applies, although to a lesser extent, in the psychological treatment of young people and adults. It also plays a role in love affairs and friendships.

Some cultures have adopted the idea that constant praise (the bountiful use of words such as "terrific," "fantastic," "outstanding," "wonderful") enhances the development of self-esteem in children as well as adults. Consequently, many people have developed in-flated egos, which is a poor substitute for a sense of "self." just as overinflated balloons are likely to pop, these "ego balloons" can explode at the slightest provocation— getting a poor report card, or breaking up with a girlfriend—leaving parents, friends, and teachers bewildered and shocked.

Definitions

Self-esteem is our knowledge about, and experience of, who we are. It addresses the question of how well we know ourselves and how we look upon what we know. Self-esteem can be envisioned as a kind of inner pillar, center, or core.

People who have a healthy, well-developed sense of self-esteem feel self-contained, at ease with themselves. Described from within, the healthy self-esteem says, "I am all right, and I am of value just because I exist!" In contrast, those with low self-esteem constantly feel uncertain, self-critical, and guilty – although their actual behavior might seem very self-promoting.

Fig 2

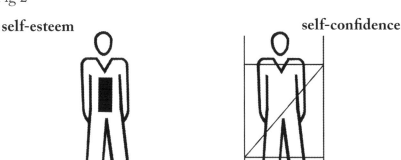

self-esteem   self-confidence

To describe the roots of self-esteem from another angle, think of new parents looking at their sleeping newborn child. They are suffused with the sense that this new human being is wonderful and precious, simply because she exists! Most parents are able to hang on to this feeling for at least several weeks. Then they begin to feel the urge to "correct" their creation. Often this need to tinker persists, overshadowing their original delight, until the child's well-being is threatened. Only when faced with the horrible possibility of losing their child do parents remember what it's like to love her just because she's herself.

Self-esteem, whether high or low, is an existential quality. It is one of the cornerstones of our psychological existence and changes throughout our lives. Both its quality and its quantity can be diminished or enhanced.

Self-confidence is a measure of what we are capable of—what we are good and clever at, or awkward and inefficient at doing. It refers to what we can achieve. Self-confidence is, as the illustration on page 85 shows, more of an acquired, external quality—although not external in the sense of being superficial.

As I have said, self-esteem and self-confidence are different concepts. They cannot really be compared to or replace each other. But they are connected: if one has a healthy self-esteem, then self-confidence is rarely a problem. The opposite, however, is certainly not the case!

If a child or adult with a well-developed sense of self-esteem attempts to learn to play the piano, for example, she will react in a levelheaded manner on discovering that she is not particularly musically inclined. She may be sad about having to give up a dream or ambition, but she will be able to express her disappointment in down-to-earth terms: "That's just not me!" Perhaps she will be able to take a completely objective perspective and say, "I just don't have the musical ability."

But a person with low self-esteem will react in a much more dramatic fashion: "I'm no good at anything!" To him, his inability to play piano is not just a question of limited musical ability; rather, he views the entire experience—in fact, his whole identity—as a fiasco.

Clearly, there is a world of difference between knowing that one is not good at a particular endeavor and feeling that one is stupid, a failure, or wrong. For one thing, it is very difficult to learn anything new when one feels stupid.

A healthy self-esteem means that one has a sober, nuanced and accepting self-image. It has nothing to do with morality or achievement, so-called strong sides and weak sides, being wonderful or terrible. It has to do with being content with *who* I am – no judgement given and no sentence passed.

I draw this distinction between self-confidence and self-esteem for an important reason. There is nothing wrong with trying to shore up one's self-confidence if one has a low sense of self-esteem. Neither should parents and other adults stop trying to build up the self-confidence of those children who have low self-esteem. But it is important not to delude ourselves into thinking that bolstering a child's self-confidence also bolsters his self-esteem. How capable we feel does not make us feel better about who we are. These are separate issues. It is good to train, develop, praise, criticize, encourage, and support people's ability to achieve—but their well-being needs tending as well.

Example: john, thirty-eight, a former national soccer champion, is now an alcoholic in treatment for his condition. He is having a disagreement with his therapists. They have suggested that he start a soccer-training program for young people from the town as part of his rehabilitation. He rejects this idea outright, claiming that he is completely finished with soccer.

His therapists interpret this as another indication of his lack of self-confidence and intensify their attempts to motivate him. Finally, john is able to express himself more clearly: "One of the reasons I started drinking was that I became very disappointed when I stopped being an active athlete. I discovered that all the people I had thought of as my friends were only backslappers." What he discovered, in terms of the concepts we've been discussing, was,

"When I stopped being an active athlete, I felt as if people only appreciated me because of what I could do —not because of who I am."

John's story is not atypical. As a boy, he'd been encouraged by both his parents and his teachers to take up soccer because he seemed to lack self-confidence. When his special talent for the sport emerged, they did everything they could to support and develop it. They attended training, involved themselves in his club, and spent most weekends as spectators. When he began to appear in the media and secured a professional contract abroad, they shared in his pleasure.

John came into conflict with his therapists because, like his parents and trainers, they overlooked an essential quality of John's: his low sense of self-esteem. Like most other children (and adults), John could express his low self-esteem only as uncertainty in relation to actions. As a child he had often said things like, "I can't do that," "I'm no good at that," "I can't figure that out," or "That's too difficult." He was unable to say, "I don't think I'm any good!"

As an athlete, John was unique, but as a person he has many fellow sufferers: children and young people who, because they believe in the wisdom of the adults surrounding them, feel as if they are only important if they can achieve something. In this way self-confidence resembles what we usually call "status symbols", which might boost your social status but it does not change who you are and how you relate to yourself.

Low self-esteem manifests itself in a great variety of ways: fear of failure, boasting, fear of life, self-effacement, boundlessness, defeatism, pompousness, feelings of guilt, use of abusive substances, violent behavior, digestive complaints, and so forth. Many of these manifestations will be considered later in this book.

I do not consider lack of self-confidence, which is not linked with low self-esteem, to be a particular problem. To put it another way, low self-confidence or its lack is not a psychological problem, but a practical pedagogical problem that can be solved with the aid of learning,training, objective feedback—from a trainer if one is involved in sports, from a publisher if one is a writer, from a colleague if one is an educator, from a teacher if one is a pupil. Self-confidence increases with the quality of the achievement.

"WATCH ME, MOM!": RECOGNIZING CHILDREN'S NEED TO BE SEEN

Our self-esteem is nurtured by two experiences: when one of the most important people in our lives "sees" and acknowledges us as we are, and when we sense that we are of value to other people as we are. These two perceptions—and fluency in a personal language, which I will discuss later in this section—are prerequisites for establishing a fruitful life on our own and together with other people.

Let me explain. In my experience, all parents love their children, but not all parents are capable of expressing their feelings equally well or relevant. Yet the expression of love is a decisive factor in the development of self-esteem. **For of what use is a parental heart swelling with love if the parent cannot behave toward the child in ways that are experienced by the child as loving?** It matters little what parents intend—what matters is what the child experiences. The same is true for adult relationships.

Little children freely acknowledge their need to be seen. In the playground, one-and-a-half-year-old Katherine takes her first ride down the slide, looks at her mother, and shouts, "Watch me, Mom!" Most parents are only too willing to watch—yet they inadvertently give the child something quite different than what the child is asking for.

For example, Katherine's mother praised her daughter by saying, "Ooh, aren't you clever! Well done!"

This comment is lovingly meant but unfortunate because it yokes "being" and "achievement." When adults converse in this way, we say that they are "speaking at cross-purposes." Suppose I invite a good friend for dinner and as we sip our coffee after the meal I say, "How nice it is to see you again!" only to have him answer, "Yes, you've certainly learned how to cook!" Clearly, we are engaged in two different conversations.

This is how Katherine feels—as if she and her mother are not communicating with each other. The girl never considered that she might need to be clever to have fun on the slide. She is in the midst of an experience, and when she says, "Watch me!" she is asking to have her experience and her existence confirmed—nothing more, nothing less. What she really wants to say is, "See me!"

Other parents express their love in a more self-centered way by saying, "Be careful now that you don't fall and hurt yourself." This type of perennial worrying poisons the development of self-esteem because the message the child receives is, "I don't expect that you can manage." It also draws the child's attention away from his own experience and focuses it on his mother's feelings. If the mother is generally worried, her son will almost certainly cooperate, either by becoming reluctant and anxious (straightforward cooperation) or by becoming clumsy and accident-prone or a dare-devil, thus living up to the mother's negative expectations (inverted cooperation).

What can parents do in this situation to feed their child's self-esteem? All Katherine's mother needs to do is establish brief eye contact, wave, and say, "Hi, Katherine!" In this way, she would indicate that she witnessed her daughter's experience. Katherine, in turn, would receive an important piece of information: she knows she has been "seen." This would satisfy her need to be loved, and to have this love communicated to her.

But suppose Katherine's mother wanted to give her child more than this acknowledgment. In that case, she could have looked closely at her daughter's face, and if she saw pure delight, she could have said, "Katherine, that looks like great fun!" If delight was mixed with fear on her daughter's face, she could say, "That looks like great fun . . . but it's dangerous too, isn't it?" What she's doing now is giving her daughter an expression—or personal language—for her inner experience. And possessing a personal language is, as I mentioned above, the third prerequisite to the development of healthy self-esteem. But children only acquire a personal language when their parents take the time to look at them and verbalize their expressions and feelings with empathy.

In other words, children need to be "seen" before they can learn to express their being verbally. Babies who can only express them-selves by means of sounds and movement of their major muscles depend on their parents to figure out what motivates their expressions. Crying, after all, can mean, "I'm frustrated," "I'm unhappy," "I'm hungry," "I'm cold," or "I'm sick." It's a parent's job to figure out which description fits each type of cry. Even when children are infants, it is important that we look them in the eye and say, "Ah, you're cold, my little one," or "Oh, you were just hungry." Sarah, whom we met in Chapter 2, would have benefited greatly if her mother had stopped trying to push food in her mouth and said, "I see that you're not hungry anymore."

Why is it so important to give children a personal language through which they can understand and express their feelings and experiences? **All conflicts between people who mean something to each other can be resolved only through the use of a personal language.** If we cannot express ourselves in personal terms, we become confused about who we ourselves are, and it becomes difficult for others to know where they stand with us.

Let's look ahead a few years, to Sarah at age four. If by that time she has developed a personal language, she will be able to say, after eating a certain amount of dinner, "No thank you, I'm not hungry anymore." If, instead, her mother has persisted in pressuring and manipulating her, she may react in a less articulate way, by pushing the plate away and saying, "I don't want it!" or "I don't like it!"—or something similarly boorish. In this situation, she has only learned two ways of reacting: to identify herself with her mother's feelings and needs, or to reject them. Either way, she has lost contact both with her own feelings and needs and with her ability to express them. Not only will this loss of contact create conflicts between Sarah and her mother as Sarah grows up, but it will undoubtedly create problems in her social relations with friends, with the man or woman she falls in love with, and with the children whom she herself may have one day.

Does this sound extreme? It is! It is one of the serious problems that result when families praise extrinsic values, such as the need to finish all the food on one's plate. In such families, personal language is either discouraged or tolerated only when children are young. As they grow, personal language is replaced by "nice" social language, which is completely unsuitable for coping with personal or interpersonal problems.

Example: Marco, a sixth grader, seems less happy and interested in school than he had been in the past. His parents are faced with two possibilities: they can attempt to "bring him up" in the traditional way, or they can attempt to "see" him.

If they choose the first option, they will say things like, "Marco, why do we have to remind you about your homework all the time? You know it has to be done! You know you can't get good grades if you don't do your homework." This old-fashioned approach totally ignores the boy as a person.

Or they could say, "Marco, what's the matter? You usually take care of homework yourself without us having to stay on top of things for you. Are you having problems at school? Are some of the other students teasing you? Is anything wrong?"

These comments express interest in the boy himself, but usually elicit responses like, "It's nothing," "No, it's just that stupid home-work," or some similarly vague reply. There are two reasons for this kind of response. In the first place, it is difficult for an eleven year-old to express inner feelings while attempting to answer concrete questions. Second, the way in which the parents express themselves communicates, "You are a problem for us. We like you better when you are happy." This represents a loss for Marco's self-esteem: instead of learning more about himself and his own life, he experiences his own feelings as being a problem. In addition, he is not given the opportunity to express his feelings in a personal language, which could accomplish two things—it could release him from his mood, and it could enable him to reveal his true self to his parents so they could learn more about him.

If Marco's parents really want to "see" their son, they only have to describe what they actually see and offer their attention: "I can see that you are having problems with your schoolwork right now, Marco. Have you thought about the reasons why?" It is possible that the answer will still be a "No," but his parents can follow up with, "I'd like to hear about it. Do you need help with your homework?" In this way, the problem has neither been defined nor solved—but that is not important at this point. What is very significant is that Marco feels as if he has been seen and that his attention is being focused in the right direction: inwardly, toward himself. Perhaps he will find words to describe what is going on with him later on that day, or perhaps not until several days have passed. Often children—like adults—need time to consider and reflect.

Example:

Sophie, who is five years old, has been given a large bag of candy by the family's weekend guests. Delighted, she walks around the apartment stuffing herself with one delicious mouthful after another. Her parents are now faced with the same choice that Marco's faced: should they "see" Sophie or educate her?

Should they just look lovingly at her and say, "You like eating a lot of sweets one right after another, don't you, Sophie?" Or should they say, "Sophie! Take one more sweet and give me the bag, so you have some left for tomorrow!" Or should they opt for the more pedagogical version: "Sophie . . . don't you think you should save some for tomorrow?"

The last two comments are not just superfluous; they have the added insidious effect of ruining Sophie's sense of sensual well being and her experience of being a part of the community of her family. In time, she will naturally learn how many sweets to eat on her own. Her parents' comments are for their sake, not Sophie's. Saying what they said allowed them to feel useful, as if they secured their reputation as responsible parents in the eyes of their guests.

The examples that I have mentioned are simple in that we as parents only need to "see" what in fact we do see. It becomes more difficult when our own history, prejudices, ideologies, and self-centeredness intervene as a filter between our retina and our vocal cords; when our attitudes and ideas get in the way of our love and openness. This happens especially when the behavior of children and young people is distorted by frustration and pain. At these times, what they need most is to be seen as they are, and not be judged.

"She is only seeking attention" we often say about behavior that we dislike and/or don't understand. In a similar way many parents say, "But children crave so much attention!" In a very direct sense this is true and fortunately they crave much more than they actually need. What the attention-seeking behavior is actually expressing is a frustrated need to be *seen* for which no amount of attention, praise or criticism can compensate.

ACKNOWLEDGMENT AND ASSESSMENT

Years ago, as I have said earlier, the objective of child rearing was primarily to get children to obey, adapt, and behave nicely. Self-esteem was barely mentioned, and concern about children's self-confidence arose only when they encountered difficulties learning in school. The "self" of the coming industrial worker was not an issue.

Back in the 1930s, educators and psychologists started to take an interest in children who were seen as lacking self-confidence, and concluded that this lack was due to the fact that their parents constantly corrected and criticized them. In my view, the diagnosis was wrong and the conclusion incomplete. The children who were examined may have lacked self-confidence, but their real problem was that they had low self-esteem.

But the experts were correct in realizing that criticism destroys both children's self-esteem and their self-confidence. As I mentioned earlier, praise and criticism are both relevant for the development of self-confidence under certain circumstances, but the idea that praise is beneficial for the development of a healthy sense of self-esteem stems from a basic misunderstanding. In fact, in terms of self-esteem, praise can be just as destructive as criticism. This is not to say that parents should suddenly be forbidden from praising their children. It simply means that we must learn to nourish children's self-esteem, and we can do this through acknowledging them. Here's an example.

Example: Three-and-a-half-year-old Larry is sitting at the kitchen table waiting for his mother who has not yet come home from work. His father suggests that Larry draw in order to pass the time. One hour and six drawings later, his mother comes home. Larry runs to the front door and gives her his latest drawing, saying, "Look, Mom, this is for you!"

His mother takes the drawing, looks at it, and says, "That's really good, Larry. How talented you are at drawing!"

Even though his mother lovingly praised his picture, Larry feels as Katherine did—that he has not made contact with his mother, that there is no connection between them. From Larry's point of view, he didn't go running to his mother with a drawing to have it assessed. He was giving his mother a gift because he loves her and missed her. If he had been looking at a picture book with his father instead of drawing when his mother came home, he would have asked his mother to look at the pictures in the book; if he had been watching television, he probably would have said, "Mom, Mom, come and look!"

The point is that he is giving himself—his immediate existence—to his mother. But in response to his spontaneous, personal expression, he receives an assessment. In this situation, it makes no difference whether the assessment is positive or negative.

If Larry's mother had been aware how to nurture her son's self-esteem, she might have acknowledged his gift and said, "Thank you, Larry. I'm pleased to have that." Or "Thank you, Larry . . . I can't really see what it's meant to be. Can you tell me?" Or "Hi, sweetie. I've missed you too!" In fact, she can say just about anything—as long as she gives him her spontaneous, personal reaction.

Of course, Larry's mother does not withhold her personal reaction because she wishes to cheat her son. On the contrary, she does it partly because she has learned that that is the way to talk to children if you want to be loving and give them self-confidence. Her knowledge about how to interact with her child originates from her own childhood, during which children were not recognized as being exactly like adults—just smaller. But if her husband talked to her in the same way that she spoke to Larry, she would eventually feel lonely and patronized.

For his part, Larry is uncomfortable with his mother's remark, but he loves his mother and feels that she loves him, so he cooperates! After a short while, he stops offering her drawings and other creations by saying, "Look, Mom, see what I made for you!" Now that he has learned the rules of the game, he says, "Look, Mom, isn't it good?" Or "Look, Mom, aren't I clever?" His perspective in life has changed from "being" to "being able to"—from being to doing, from existence to achievement.

It is easier, perhaps, to understand the problem I'm describing if we think about what would have happened if Larry's mother had criticized his drawing instead of praising it. If she had said, "But Larry, you know how to draw a house properly!" Or "What's that, Larry? You can do that much better!" we would easily recognize instantly how hurtful her comments were.

Pleasure and pain are momentary emotional reactions, but they have a lasting effect on children's personality if the criticism is daily and massive.

The danger of loving one's children by means of either praise or criticism is the fact that this approach has long-term effects on the development of personality. By focusing on praise and criticism, we produce dependent, extrinsically controlled personalities. Children brought up by this method have low self-esteem, lack the ability to evaluate themselves, and waste their vitality in the sometimes lifelong attempt to be liked, to make their parents proud of them and to act according to how they perceive they are expected to behave. In addition, they tend to become extremely self-centered in their constant pursuit of acknowledgment.

From about 1700 up to the 1950s, criticism was the most important instrument of power that adults could wield. This is still the case in some families; in fact, some societies uphold the theory that children can only become good people if they are continually told how wrong they are. In many Western countries, the new methods of preschool education that flourished after World War II rejected the use of criticism and introduced praise as a controlling mechanism. This is how our brain works – it thinks in opposites instead of alternatives if we don't educate it.

Some families prefer to have extrinsically controlled children just as some societies favor extrinsically controlled citizens, but from the mental health point of view this is an unfortunate preference. I consider self-esteem to be an existential mechanism of immunity: when it is well developed, we are happier, less vulnerable, have more satisfying relationships, and enjoy a better quality of life.

Many parents can appreciate the value of this more contemporary approach yet remain nervous that they will lose their power within the family. Further, they are afraid that they will be unable to define the framework and norms that children need if they are to develop in a healthy way. As I will soon explain, parents need not have such fears. The only power that parents must relinquish is their dictatorial power and their power-of-definition – i.e. their right to define who and what the child is instead of helping him express and thereby define him self.

In the example of Larry and his mother, I described one form of acknowledgment: the spontaneous, personal reaction. Another form, which I will describe next, is the more thoughtfully considered personal response. (*The phenomenn of acknowledgment or recognition can be difficult to grasp in the English language. It originates from the German "Anerkennung" which has a slight different ring to it*).

GIVING CHILDREN A SENSE OF VALUE

In keeping with tradition, we often think and act as if our relationship with children is a one-way street on which the traffic flows from us to them. Modern parents are also continually preoccupied with the question about whether they are giving their children enough— enough attention, love, togetherness, stimulation, care, and a sense of possibility.

This is all very well—as long as we remember that children's self-esteem also relies to a great extent on the degree to which they experience that they are of value to our lives. The more we allow them to give us, the healthier their self-esteem becomes. There are many joys connected with having children: we thrill to their smiles, devotion, interest, caring, and curiosity. When they bring us breakfast in bed, do well at school or in a sport, marry, present us with grandchildren, come to visit us, we are pleased— and it is important to show how pleased we are. But these are all superficial examples of what children can give to parents.

When I talk of children's gifts, I think of the actual existential challenges with which all children present their parents—because they are who they are. Children force us to consider our own self-destructive patterns; they take us beyond the limit of pain and make us think about whether we are suitable to be parents in the first place; they expose our shallow, pedagogical attempts at manipulation and insist on our personal presence; they offend us by rejecting our good advice and guidance; they proudly and matter of-factly assert their right to be different; they act in destructive ways that force us to confront the fact that we have slipped up. To put it briefly: their unique competence makes such a great impression on us that we either have to acknowledge it or lie to ourselves.

Like so many of us who have grown up with very little self-esteem, I often encounter problems in finding out "who I really am." I fluctuate between being either self-effacing or pompous— in varying degrees. Not surprisingly, my son has always been most offended by my pompousness. Those of us who have a hard time taking ourselves seriously often end up exaggerating our seriousness to the point of caricature. Of course, behaving this way isn't helpful, to ourselves or to others.

I recall three episodes in particular when my son lovingly, yet without mercy, deflated my balloon.

During the first two years of his life, I often felt very uncertain about what I should do with him and with myself. This uncertainty, combined with my natural tendency to be temperamental, caused me to vent my frustration by shouting at him on occasion. Naturally, he was overwhelmed and frightened, but I did not know what to do about it.

When he turned two, however, and was able to get around by himself, he put a stop to my completely unreasonable behavior. In the middle of one of my discharges, he ran out of the room and into the hall. Of course, I went after him. I found him on the staircase—on the fourth step, to be precise—so that we were at eye level. His hands were over his ears, and he glared at me with real anger and said, "Stop it now!" At that moment, I realized that perhaps I should take responsibility for my incompetence instead of blaming him for it.

Fast-forward ten years. As a twelve-year-old, he had a burning interest in snakes and reptiles. One day he came home beaming and told me that the father of one of his friends had offered him a young python for his collection. "I'd really like to have it," he said. "May I?"

Since he knew that his mother had grown up with reptiles as pets, and that I had a moderate phobia about snakes, he addressed his question exclusively to me. It was difficult to say yes, and even more difficult to say no, so I asked for some time to think about it. I told him I'd give him my answer when I returned from teaching a forthcoming weekend course.

On Saturday I came home for lunch to find my son busily sawing and hammering in the garage. "What are you making?" I asked.

"A terrarium!" he replied.

"For what?" I asked.

"For the snake, of course!" he replied.

Neurotic or not, I felt that this called for a little fatherly firmness:

"But we haven't finished discussing that, Nicolai!"

"I know that. I reckon that you'll say what you've decided, when you've made up your mind."

Lovingly and considerately, I was given another (well-earned) lesson in equal dignity. Because my son knew what he wanted, he felt free to pursue his goal; at the same time, he fully expected that I would figure out what I wanted and inform him of my decision when I did.

The most recent episode took place six months after he had left home. My wife and I were planning a large garden party for friends and family, and I asked Nicolai if he would come home and be responsible for serving the food. (I must add here that I am a passionate cook—and prone to temper tantrums, particularly when I prepare large or important dinners.) "I'll have to think about it," he said. Two days later, he called to say, "Okay, I'd like to. When shall I come?"

The party began well enough. My son arranged and set a beautiful table, reserving a seat for himself beside mine, and served the first two courses. When I finally took a break and came to join the party, he sat by my side. I could have appreciated his company and all his hard work. Instead I made a quick survey of the tables and said, "The plates need changing, NOW, Nicolai!" He froze, and his eyes turned black as coal. After a brief moment of hesitation, he looked at me in exactly the same way as he had that time on the stairs and said, "What do I get for it?"

My initial reaction was, "What do you mean, payment? You help your parents without expecting to be paid! Just think of what we have given you. . . ." My next thought was to consider his behavior as a "sign of the times"—always a good explanation—and I thought to myself, "It's getting a bit too much these days, the way young people think they can talk to us as equals!" Finally, in an apotheosis of self-importance, I felt resentful: "He must realize how much this party means to me!" Luckily for both of us—and our relationship—I didn't voice any of these thoughts aloud.

This time twenty-four hours passed before I realized that I had made an ass of myself. When it dawned on me, I felt ashamed for the first time in many years. I had asked him to do me a friendly favor, and he had offered to help as a friend. In a moment of colossal self-centeredness, I had spoken to him as if he was a hired hand. No wonder he had demanded payment!

We all receive hundreds of these gold nuggets every day when we spend time with our children. It is important both for our children's and our own self-esteem that we acknowledge them by means of a verbal response and a change in behavior as soon as possible—preferably, on the spot, but if not, later that day or even ten years later.

Foster families, or families with children who are physically or mentally handicapped, need to be particularly aware of the dual sources of self-esteem—being seen and feeling valued. For children with special needs, their development of self-esteem can easily be blocked by the fact that they experience themselves as being a "burden" for or a "project" of their parents. There are a number of reasons for this.

Handicapped children, restricted by the more or less narrow limits that determine what they can achieve intellectually or physically, depend on help from their parents. Asking for help, whether one is handicapped, elderly, infirm, a refugee, or living on public assistance, is demoralizing to a person's self-esteem.

Handicapped children also run the risk of not being "seen" but just being looked at. In addition, because their potential for doing things is limited, they often have difficulty experiencing themselves as being of value to their parents.

Thus the parents of handicapped children need to be honest and personal in their spontaneous reactions to the child—even when they feel irritated, disheartened, and exhausted. These parents also need to respond to their children in terms of their being, not their achievement. Many parents, afraid that they might hurt their child, are reluctant to do so, and instead channel their own and the child's attention on what the child can achieve. This is good for the child's self-confidence and can reduce the child's physical dependence, but it does not nourish the child's self-esteem. In fact, most of the signals and responses that nourish a child's sense of self-esteem can be given regardless of age or disability.

Infants, of course, do not feel undignified because they depend on others; they accept love, care, and food as a matter of course. But children who are just slightly older, and those who lose their daily contact with their biological parents through adoption or foster care, no longer take their care for granted. They are completely aware that others are doing what biological parents do, and they quickly feel indebted to these adults.

Most children in this situation can't verbally express these feelings of gratitude until they themselves become adults. As children and teens, their feelings often surface as aggression, reticence, or an exaggerated desire to adapt or cooperate. This type of behavior can serve as a reminder to parents that they have been too obsessed with the idea of giving and that they need to sit back and start receiving.

"Invisible" Children

Some children grow up in families in which they are "invisible," which is to say that they are never "seen" as they are and as they feel. This can be the case throughout their entire childhood and adolescence, or just during particular periods, such as puberty.

Example:

Earlier, I mentioned Alecia, whom I met because her parents had requested a consultation. At thirteen, she was extremely over-weight, and a veteran of many diets: it was her weight problem that had led the parents to seek help.

When she blurted out, "The only thing you can see is my flesh!" she reminded her parents how important it is for those who love us to "see" us. Luckily for Alecia, she is one of those young people who has a healthy fighting spirit and the capacity to express herself. Many young people of her age would not have been able to protest so vehemently and accurately. They would have sat passively and shyly on their chair while the adults discussed their symptoms.

Alecia belongs to a category of children (and adults) who are not "seen," but only looked at. In her situation, this occurred because she was overweight, but it could just as well have been because she was underweight, handicapped, strikingly beautiful, or conspicuous for any other reason.

In cases like this, adults often make one of two mistakes. Sometimes we are guilty of focusing on the "surface"—which is exactly what we fear other children will do. Worried that our overweight daughter will be teased, which will erode her self-confidence, we pour our loving and committed energy into helping her lose weight—thereby creating the same situation that we are trying to protect her from! Inadvertently, our insistent concern makes her feel as self-conscious as sarcasm or teasing.

The other mistake we often make is that we revert to oversimplified psychological interventions and explanations that stress underlying problems. This is quite understandable because logic is deceptive. Here is an example. We might conclude that an overweight young boy eats compulsively because he is unhappy about something. If we can discover the source of his unhappiness, he will stop overeating.

Yet life is rarely that simple. People gorge or starve themselves for many reasons—among them, specific, time-limited problems that they cannot solve on their own. In most cases, their greatest pain arises because they do not feel "seen." That pain was present long before they started to develop visible symptoms.

Instead of treating these symptoms and/or becoming a problem-solving detective, I suggest that we think in a new, more demanding but rewarding way. The self-destructive behavior of children represents only a part of who they are. Another part of them is healthy and vigorous—which implies that they are also unreasonable, irrational, exuberant, angry, unhappy, childish, irritating, demanding, and active. But they have slowly lost touch with their healthy, original selves. It started with the feeling that the healthy part was not welcome in the family, and eventually culminated in a condition that couldn't be ignored. In the conflict between the person's healthy and unhealthy sides, the healthy side has been defeated.

Our task, then, is clear—to help them recover the healthy and vigorous part of themselves and invite them back into the bosom of the family where they have not felt welcome for a long time. This is the only way that we can nourish children's self-esteem in the long term.

If, on the other hand, we try to combat the unhealthy part by using so-called motivation, force, or criticism, we will succeed only in limiting the power the unhealthy self has established. The unhealthy part is pushed back without the healthy part being encouraged to come forth. Our efforts may seem successful at first, but success of this type comes at a high price because people who act in self-destructive ways come to know themselves as self-destructive, without becoming acquainted with any of their healthy parts.

In other words, children often develop signals that adults misinterpret as attention-getting devices, and then they pay attention to the signals. What the children are really asking, however, is to be "seen" as they really are and feel inside—a desire that they are unable to express in direct, personal language.

WHY CHILDREN BECOME "INVISIBLE"

Children become "invisible" in their families for many different reasons. Some parents—such as those who think that children should learn to "behave themselves" and who do not believe in the importance of children learning to "be themselves"—make an active attempt to shape their children in a particular way. But the same problem occurs in more flexible, modern families in which demands for "reasonableness" and "common sense" are so prominent that children quickly learn to dissociate themselves from their more unreasonable and irrational sides.

It can also happen in families where the parents' married life is so problematic and dramatic that the children conclude there is no room for them. Other cases occur when a child is completely different from her older sisters and brothers, and this difference is perceived as a problem. It is not unusual for children who have a handicapped brother or sister, or children who are raised by one parent who feels especially overburdened, to feel invisible too.

Children and young people become "invisible" in their families if they have, from an early age, been allocated a particular role ("Dad's little princess," "the bright or easy-going one," "trouble," "the family introvert," or "the family clown").

Example: Fourteen-year-old Lisa lives with her mother, stepfather, and two younger sisters. She is a pretty, clever girl who is doing well at school. She has no close friends and has never had any—a fact that she herself regrets but is not particularly unhappy about.

The family requested counseling because of Lisa. Within the garrulous family, she is considered "odd," "peculiar," and "strange." She frustrates the others with her silence. She says very little on her own initiative and gives one-syllable answers when questioned.

Lisa has recently asked her parents if she can move away from home "to a boarding school or something like that." Her parents are not against the idea, but ask Lisa why she wants to move away from home. Here they come up against their perennial problem with Lisa: she cannot answer this kind of personal question.

This problem has become entrenched over the years. Whenever Lisa's parents ask her a question—for example, "Is there anything you are dissatisfied with?"—Lisa thinks carefully and attempts to find the right words that express what she feels in a way that her parents will understand. But before she is able to, her parents lose patience and ask again, "Do you think we demand too much of you at home? Are you having problems at school? Lisa, is there anything in particular that you are unhappy about?"

Sensing their impatience and their helplessness, Lisa feels ashamed that she has so much difficulty in expressing herself in words. In order to escape being the center of attention, she answers, "No!" Naturally, this answer further frustrates her parents, who are doing their best to be solicitous. The situation is certainly no less unpleasant for Lisa herself. Like all other children and young people in this situation, she concluded a long time ago that since her beloved parents are perfect, there must be something wrong with her.

Sometime later, Lisa finds an answer to her parents' question. She says, "I think that perhaps I will be more able to find myself if I live away from home"—an incredibly insightful and truthful answer. In actuality, Lisa has been "invisible" within her family nearly all her life. Yet because her parents have been caring and committed in so many other ways, her integrity has never really been harmed, and she has been able to keep "herself" intact. The real Lisa exists somewhere inside her, together with the longing to be "seen." She has given up hope that her parents will "see" her and is therefore hoping that by going away she will be able to "find herself."

Lisa's difficulties expressing her self personally are closely related to her "invisibility." When she is invited to speak, and when people are patient, she is able to say more than she usually does, but only with great hesitation and uncertainty. All her life, her behavior and moods have been wrongly interpreted. She has been convinced that she is as her parents see her, not as she has experienced herself from within. With each passing day, she naturally becomes more and more reluctant to allow her (wrong) inner "self" to be heard.

But Lisa wasn't the only one in pain. Her mother had constant feelings of guilt about their lack of closeness and contact, whereas her stepfather felt frustrated that Lisa perpetually rejected his goodwill and interest. Lisa's plan was realistic: she knew that the only way to successfully establish contact between herself and her family was to find herself in her own way. She needed to practice expressing herself around people who did not have preconceptions about her.

Luckily for Lisa, she was able to find a solution for herself while she was still a teenager. Many people like her do not realize their situation until well after they have become adults. Some children, at a very early stage in their lives, give up their attempts to be seen, and as a consequence they isolate themselves from their parents and assume the existential responsibility for themselves. This group will be described in Chapter 5.

From Invisible To Visible

What should parents do when they realize that they have an "invisible" child, a child whose individual, personal being they have been unable to "see" for whatever reason? How can they restructure the family to include a child who has been emotionally excluded?

First, forgive yourself and each other! And I mean forgiveness in the good old-fashioned sense of the word—where we give ourselves time to face up to our culpability and responsibility, and look each other in the eye—not the quick, discount type of forgiveness common today, which involves forgetting the past and starting all over again. In situations like this, people need to commit themselves to learning something new—about their child, their family, and themselves.

This process takes time, but is critical if the child is to develop healthy self-esteem. If feelings of guilt either predominate or are repressed, the child will pick up on this as a signal, and will misinterpret it to mean, "My parents think they have been bad parents. That must mean that they are not satisfied with me as I am. Otherwise they wouldn't feel guilty about it." When children perceive that their parents feel guilty, their self-esteem diminishes even more, and all the constructive actions parents take are often futile.

Families should also adhere to their traditions. If, for example, the family has a history of doing many things together, it should continue to do so; if members are more independent, that tradition should continue as well. Parents who want to use this opportunity of reincorporating an invisible child as a time to change family dynamics should do so because *they* are unhappy with the way things are—not merely "for the child's sake."

The more difficult challenge parents face is to imagine that they are living with a completely unknown child, a child who experiences reality in a different way from everyone else, and who in many ways does not resemble the child they have "known" for the past five, ten, or fifteen years. Parents have to shed their older conceptions of the child and meet her as openly and flexibly as possible. And this process has to be undertaken not in the spirit of sacrifice, but in such a manner that the child knows that her parents are prepared to modify their usual limits and boundaries and include her in their lives in new ways.

Remember, the child's innermost "self" that has lived in hiding for so long will feel exposed and vulnerable. The process of becoming "visible" again takes time. It may be years before a child develops enough self-esteem and trust in other people to dare to express his or her innermost thoughts and feelings. This does not mean that parents have to tread softly, but they should refrain from criticism, reprimands, and righteousness. Suppressing these kinds of remarks will inevitably benefit the whole family.

Violence Is Violence Is Violence!

Integrity and self-esteem are related. The more successfully parents look after a child's integrity, the greater the possibility that the child will develop healthy self-esteem. Violence, as mentioned earlier, is an infringement of children's integrity and therefore detrimental to their self-esteem.

The fact that we have laws that forbid grievous physical violence against children does not mean that other forms of violence are not harmful: we have simply decided that these manifestations of violence should not be classified as unlawful.

Over time, we have coined many synonyms for physical violence. In Denmark we refer to a parent's "right to inflict corporal punishment" and talk about "smacks" or "slaps." In the United States, parents talk about "disciplining" and "spanking." In short, most cultures have their own pet names that people use in order to justify the phenomenon. But no euphemism can obscure the fact that violence is violence, and that violence destroys the self-esteem and dignity of victim and perpetrator.

In my experience, parents who use violence on their children can be divided into three groups. The first group uses violence as an attitude or ideology. These parents say, "Well, I don't think that it does children any harm to get a smack on their bottom when they deserve it." If pressed, they usually admit that they didn't feel this way before they became parents, and that their change of heart reflects an attempt to make a virtue out of necessity.

Those parents for whom the use of violence represents an ideology, and who believe that violence is an essential part of responsible child rearing, often come from environments or societies that are dominated by totalitarian ideologies, whether religious or political. In such societies, the lives and the quality of life of ordinary individuals play a subordinate role; therefore the fact that violence is destructive for the individual carries little weight.

The second group consists of parents who use violence simply because they want power over their children. Their goal is control and domination; they value obedience over closeness or confuse the two.

In the third group are those parents who hit their children on occasion but feel bad about it each time.

Regardless of a parent's attitude, however, all violence toward children has exactly the same consequences as violence toward adults: it creates anxiety, mistrust, and feelings of guilt in the short term, and low self-esteem, anger, and violence in the long term. The repercussions of violence are not necessarily proportional to how often a child is hit. I have met people who had been treated violently by their parents on only one occasion in the course of their childhood and adolescence, and who have never recovered from the pain. I have also met people who have been hit frequently and who bear few scars. The factors that seem to have an impact on how seriously an act of violence will reverberate is whether the parents take responsibility for the violence or blame their children for it and whether the violence is predictable (when I do this it might happen) or unpredictable.

Example: Suppose a young mother is leaving her apartment with her eighteen-month-old son and a girlfriend. She picks up her son, puts him down a second later with a grimace, and gives him a hard slap on the back of his head. She then grabs his upper arm and drags him back into the apartment. Shocked and amazed, her girlfriend asks her why she hit her son.

The woman replies, calmly, "I just changed him half an hour ago, and now he needs changing again. He's not going to mess around with me, and he might as well learn that right now."

"But he's not even two," her girlfriend objects. "You can't expect him to be able to let you know when he wants to go."

The mother replies by repeating her earlier remark.

Not only is this expression of violence cruel, it's also the most destructive type of violence because it places the responsibility for the violence on the child: "It's your own fault that I hit you!"

This mother lives in a culture in which violence is often used and is generally accepted as a natural part of child rearing. But the fact that violence is a part of the culture does not make it impersonal. Each time he is hit, this woman's son experiences violence as a very personal message informing him that he is wrong and without value.

Naturally, the boy cried bitterly when he was hit. His initial tears were loud and panicky because of the shock and physical pain. Later, when he was being changed, he cried in a more subdued but deeper way because of his emotional pain. But despite his strong emotional reaction, his self-esteem is not yet in danger. The situation won't become dire until he is two or three, at which age he will have learned to stop expressing his feelings.

The mother reacted to her son's crying as she had to his bowel movement: she criticized, condemned, and threatened him. The boy could only conclude that his excrement was as wrong and personally insulting to his mother, as was his distress.

What's ahead for this boy? Most likely this form of violence will recur regularly, several times a week, until the boy is about ten or eleven years old. Because of the culture in which he lives, he will also be regularly subjected to a type of behavior that appears to be the opposite of violence: he will be presented to others with pride; he will be praised and doted on, and kissed and hugged. Because his self-esteem has been crushed by violence, he will be grateful for the praise and idolization, and he will eternally honor and dote on his mother. He will develop into an insistent and charming young man who, in the presence of others, will be bursting with self-confidence. And later as a husband and father he will probably perpetrate the violence he experienced during his own upbringing.

The violence he endured as a child will most likely have the following consequences:

1. Emotionally, he will repress the anxiety, pain, and humiliation from his consciousness and remember his childhood as having been happy.

2. Mentally, he will conclude that violence toward children, when the fault is theirs, is a reasonable way of bringing them up.

3. Existentially and in terms of his personality, he will suffer from low self-esteem and will be less sensitive to other people's limits. He will engage in certain self-destructive behaviors.

4. Physically, he will be plagued by specific contractions and obstructions of the back, stomach, and chest, which will parallel his general, unconscious reservation in his contact with those nearest and dearest to him. His lack of trust will be reflected in physiological tightness.

I assume a number of factors when listing these typical consequences of violence: that the boy's parents have good social standing; that they are reasonably emotionally stable and do not have drug problems; that their marriage is not dominated by physical or psychological violence; and that the boy is an average or above average achiever in school.

If one or more of these factors is missing, the boy's low self-esteem will become obvious at a much younger age. He might develop learning difficulties, behavioral problems, become involved in crime, join a gang, abuse drugs or alcohol, or attempt suicide—because his parents, through their violent actions, have taught him not to respect his own or other people's physical and psychological integrity. The fact that his parents are otherwise regular churchgoers who preach that one should love one's neighbors only serves to erode his self-esteem even further.

What about those people who do not believe in using violence, but become desperate and forget themselves now and then? Can they take action to prevent their children from being harmed by an occasional hitting or spanking?

The answer is yes! Parents can mitigate the effects of a slap if they

- calm themselves down;

- accept responsibility, emotionally and verbally;

- give their child an opportunity to be alone with his reactions;

- reestablish contact by saying, "I'm sorry that I hit you. When I did it, I thought that it was your fault. It isn't. It's my fault and I'd like to apologize."

Read this statement again and consider it. If you are in your thirties, you may think that it is a bit too much. You may think, "Of course, I am the one who is responsible. I am the adult and I should be able to think clearly. But we also need to consider the cause of the situation."

This way of thinking is not unusual. It is an echo from a not too distant past when children were automatically blamed for any conflict that arose with their parents. Even today, many parents subscribe to this view, and react in one of two ways.

In the more sentimental version, the parent says: "Come here, dear, come to Mommy. Mommy is so sorry that she hit you. It wasn't meant to happen. Come on dear, Mommy will wipe your nose and then we'll forget it all, won't we. I'll never do it again, I promise."

This sounds sweet at first, but notice that this parent does not assume responsibility for her action. She merely says, "It wasn't meant to happen," and thus does not relieve her child of blame. Second, what she says places another burden on her child because she asks for forgiveness and concludes with a promise she probably won't be able to keep, owing to her lack of self-awareness.

A more pedagogical reaction sounds like this: "I'm so sorry about that. You must forgive me. I don't know what got hold of me. But can't you understand that you were acting unreasonably? Come on, let's go out in the kitchen. It won't happen anymore, will it?"

This version attempts to share the blame fairly—and plants guilt in the souls of both parties. It's a completely universal human phenomenon: every time we either cannot or will not take responsibility for ourselves, we let ourselves down and burden both the people around us and our relationship with them. That is why I maintain that both parties involved in a violent episode are hurt by the violence. This principle applies not only to parents and children, but to people in all types of relationships.

People who perpetrate violence experience the following:

- Their feelings will always immediately tell them that they have done something wrong. Thus, In order to carry on, they will have to disregard their feelings, thereby reducing their sensitivity and human dignity. Probably, their human dignity was stunted many years ago when they themselves were the victims of violence, but the degeneration continues every time they carry out acts of violence. Inevitably, their development as a human being is either limited or comes to a standstill. Their emotional life is reduced to sentimentality.

- Mentally, their reaction can go one of two ways: they have or they assume a moral standpoint that justifies violence so that their actions and attitudes will not be in conflict. Or, as mentioned above, they disclaim all responsibility for their actions by either blaming the other party or by inventing a "being" inside themselves that they can neither contact nor control.

- Existentially, they will inevitably come to regard their own lives with the same contempt with which they treat the lives of other people. They may compensate for this state of being by paying great attention to their own physical welfare, their social life, and their material well-being. But underneath this apparent self-respect, self-destruction will prevail.

For people for whom the use of violence is the exception rather than the rule, the consequences I've just described will be pronounced but will affect perhaps only part of their existence. Perhaps they will never come into contact with this part of themselves. But the consequences are not abstract: they are completely real and proportional to the extent of the violence.

In relationships between children and adults, adults are always responsible when violence erupts. This does not just apply to those cases in which the adults use violence, but also to those in which children or young people behave violently toward their parents, brothers and sisters, friends, and strangers, and to property belonging to their immediate family or to other people.

In recent years, politicians from all over the world have come forward to condemn the violent actions of children and young people. With the support of outraged and indignant parents, they have made demands for harsher punishment. This strategy is beyond absurd. It is about as ludicrous as the suggestion that we should pay off the national deficit with Monopoly money.

Partly as a result of the liberalization of society and the increasing self-awareness among children and young people, a terrifying number of them express their pain publicly and destructively. This development will continue until we begin to assume responsibility for the massive violence, both physical and psychological, that adults still express toward children in the name of education.

Clinicians and neuro-scientists agree: Physical as well as emotional violence lowers the cognitive intelligence of children as well as

their emotional and social intelligence. It might make them quiet and easy for a while but it reduces the quality of their existence in so many ways.

Adults' Self -Esteem

Many parents ask whether it is at all possible to support their children's healthy self-esteem when they themselves suffer from low self-esteem. It is possible—if parents are prepared to make an active, conscious effort to develop their own self-esteem.

In fact, our self-esteem develops all through our lives, inasmuch as we get to know ourselves better as time goes by; that is, our self-esteem develops in quantity, but not necessarily in quality. We may know more about ourselves, but we may not necessarily regard ourselves in a different way. To improve the quality of our self-esteem—even if our self-perception is initially characterized by uncertainty, self-criticism, superficiality, or pessimism—we need to make a conscious effort.

If we do not make this conscious effort, then our lingering low self-esteem becomes a part of our children's "social" or perhaps it is more accurate to say "socio-psychological" inheritance. This tends to happen if parents are subjected to a social situation over a long period of time that causes their self-esteem to deteriorate, or saps the self-confidence they have laboriously built up to compensate for their low self-esteem. Unemployment, exile, being deprived of prestigious positions or status symbols, and physical or mental incapacity are all examples of situations that can make people feel as if they have less or no value to those around them.

As I have said, the most important contribution that parents can make within the framework of the family is to be aware of the opposition their children offer them and the impression it makes on them. For many parents this also means that they must free themselves from adhering to a number of conventions and reject the well-intentioned criticism of the rest of the family.

Our culture supports the delusion that we become adults when we reach the age of eighteen or twenty-one—or, at the very latest, when we have children of our own. As most people know, this is not true. Many of us do not even manage to become adults before we die. This does not mean that we always behave childishly, but simply that we often behave immaturely, especially in relation to those nearest to us.

There is nothing unnatural or wrong about this lack of maturity, and it does not do our children any harm. Parents don't need to have healthy self-esteem before they become parents in order to raise children with good self-esteem. But they do need to continue to develop their self-esteem, together with their children. And they can do this by acting with integrity.

Since children are challenging our beliefs, boundaries, values and emotions every day they are the ideal companions in the maturing process of their parents. By searching for truthful and authentic reactions to these challenges we all grow.

Remember, children love their parents unconditionally no matter how they are treated. The development of a child's self-esteem is important not because of how she regards her parents, but in terms of how much she likes herself.

RESPONSIBILITY, BEING RESPONSIBLE, AND POWER

Defining responsibility and describing the boundaries of responsible behavior is a major conceptual task for parents and professionals whenever they discuss how children should be raised and educated. Although these terms are more straight forward than the concepts discussed previously (self-confidence, self-value, and self-esteem), both responsibility and responsible behavior are used in many contexts.

I suggest making a distinction between "social responsibility" and "personal (existential) responsibility." Each is distinct and important in its own way, yet both are essential if we want to create relationships within the family that are based on treating one another with equal dignity, relationships that enhance everyone's integrity and self-esteem, and promote reciprocal good feelings. In my experience, our failure to distinguish between these two concepts often explains our poor track record in dealing with children and young people.

Definitions

Social responsibility (which I will explore in Chapter 5) is the responsibility we have for each other—those in our family, community, society, and the world. It enables larger groups of people—groups, societies—to function as well as they do. We learn about social responsibility from our parents and teachers.

Personal responsibility isS the responsibility we have for our own lives—our physical, psychological, mental, and spiritual health and development. Although few of us are raised to assume this responsibility, it is very powerful. When we are personally responsible, we can prevent adversity and contribute to the social well-being of the group of which we are a member.

Traditionally, child rearing and educational theories have emphasized social responsibility. More recently, however, we have discovered (or perhaps rediscovered) the close relationship between these two types of responsibility:

Fig 3

SOCIAL RESPONSIBILITY
responsibility toward family and society

PERSONAL RESPONSIBILITY
responsibility for our own life

Social responsibility is the fabric of society and personal responsibility is the fabric of individual existence and the interrelatedness between individual and society is so complex that it would be futile to make one more important than the other.

When children are brought up to be aware of their social responsibility, they often become socially responsible. In fact, many of them become what I would describe as over-responsible. Unfor-tunately, these socially overdeveloped people often lack personal responsibility, either completely or partially. On the other hand, when children are brought up to develop their natural, personal responsibility, they also tend to become highly socially responsible as a part of this process. This phenomenon completely contradicts one of the bedrock beliefs about how to bring up children: that their "egocentric nature" must be repressed out of consideration for the larger community. **It also contradicts the beliefs of those who assume that it is necessary to compromise one's own integrity in order to be of value to one's community.**

With our new understanding of the interrelationship between personal and social responsibility, it is clear that in order for children to grow up to be sensitive and considerate adults, they must live with adults who

* safeguard their personal integrity; and

* intervene when they sense that children are cooperating to an excessive degree.

By doing so, these adults ensure that children develop healthy self-esteem and a high degree of self-responsibility which in turn is a gift to any group they chose to belong to including society at large.

I estimate that for every hundred adults between the ages of twenty and forty, perhaps ten or fifteen are able to take responsibility for their own lives most of the time. The overwhelming majority of conflicts between children and adults—and among adults themselves—develop in a destructive way precisely because the parties are unable (or unwilling) to take responsibility for themselves. Instead, they misuse their energy by blaming each other. In the industrialized countries, our relatively high standard of living has prevented us from reflecting on the existential dimension of our lives over the past few decades. Only the prospect of death summons such thoughts. Not coincidentally, serious or fatal illnesses are among the most powerful sources of change, inspiring us to defy our good upbringing. Faced with death, many of us alter, in the space of a second, all of our basic priorities. We shift from being extrinsically controlled to being intrinsically controlled.

What do I mean by extrinsic control? If we look back to the values that dominated child rearing a generation ago, we will see that they were based on an external ideal: "Now, remember to behave yourself so that other people can see that you have been brought up properly!" Make your parents proud!

The instructions that my friends and I were given when we were sent out into the world informed us that we shouldn't seek to be true to ourselves but rather that we needed to "behave" ourselves as precisely as actors delivering monologues. And like actors we learned, with the help of expert instruction, to say the "right" lines by heart. Who we were and how we felt about ourselves were simply not important. It was not considered unimportant in any conscious way. It was simple not an issue. When given a Christmas present we said, "Thank you," in a nice tone of voice, concealing any disappointment or upset. Not until children learned to conceal "themselves," and subsequently lost contact with themselves, could parents begin to relax in the knowledge that their children's upbringing had been successfully completed.

This core belief—that the goal of raising children was to make them conform to an external ideal—is an old one, arising generations ago, when children were considered a social necessity; they were seen as members of the workforce who would be responsible for providing for their parents when they retired or got sick. Later children became, among other things, social manifestations of the morals, ambitions, and status of their parents. By the 1950s we gradually acknowledged that children were human beings who deserved to be treated with dignity, and who had the right to their own personal growth and development. Today we are still adjusting to the idea that not only do children have an existence separate from ours, but also that it is of value in itself—that children are unique and valuable simply because they exist!

In short, the status of children has undergone a radical change in the space of just over a hundred years—a shift in values, from stressing extrinsic, social values to stressing those values that are more intrinsic and existential. Naturally, during the process of trying to implement this shift in values into everyday life, some of our efforts will fail. Sometimes we go overboard in our efforts. Fifty years ago, for example, a father who disowned his son because of the son's refusal to follow in his father's footsteps would have received society's approbation. But today we see parents who bend over backward in the opposite direction: parents are so careful not to infringe on their children's rights to self-development and authonomy that their children actually grow up in a parentless vacuum. Some people—for different reasons in different cultures—confuse self-development with ego expansion.

The story of individual versus society is the ongoing story about the conflict between integrity and cooperation. There is not solution to this conflict. We can only seek a relative balance that seems satisfying for the moment

In recent years, many people have been concerned about what they experience as an increasing tendency toward individualism. I know that many parents share this concern—even those who want to give their children greater opportunities for development than they themselves had. They desire to support a dimension of their children's development that they themselves have only come into contact with at a great personal cost.

It is easy to understand their concerns. News flashes from the "global village" are filled with violence, with reports of quick-changing trends. Parents are also concerned about the divorce rate, statistics regarding rape and suicide, and the fact that some schoolchildren now carry weapons. (From a certain perspective, the emergence of "virtual reality" is a godsend.)

Understandably, many people ask themselves whether "all that freedom" is good for children. But these people confuse personal responsibility with personal license. In fact, personal, or existential responsibility, which I define as fundamentally necessary for healthy interaction between people, has nothing to do with the concerns mentioned above.

I do not believe that our new insight into the factors that are most beneficial for healthy human development has polarized relations between people. It is difficult to imagine how relationships between children and adults that are based on equal dignity could create problems of this kind. More likely, irresponsibility, greed and self sufficiency underlie our current problems.

The First Step is the Hardest

Parents who want to give their children a more balanced start in life are forced to experiment. The degree to which one experiments is influenced by a number of personal experiences and cultural biases. Differences exist between countries, and within countries. Mass communication via satellite TV, the Internet, and film may distribute new knowledge and ideas quickly and effectively, but the ground on which they fall differs vastly.

In the former Iron Curtain countries, where populations have been subjected to extreme, totalitarian regimes, the concept of individual, personal responsibility had almost ceased to exist. For over half a century, people have become accustomed to the idea that the individual is of no importance and that personal initiative is a political crime against the state. The mere idea that a person can assume responsibility for his or her quality of life seems to most people an abstract thought. These experiences from life in a totalitarian state are quite similar to those a Danish child would have encountered one or two generations ago. Both would hear comments such as: "It's no good saying anything," "What could I have done? You couldn't do anything!" and "How can you take a child seriously?"

At the other extreme is the United States, where individual initiative has always been emphasized. American families (if it is at all possible to talk about "an American family" in a multicultural society of this kind), however, are filled with contradictions. On the one hand, many families struggle to maintain certain antiquated family values and symbols; on the other, they define individuality as loneliness and perceive both demanding emotional relations as well as personal commitments as limitations on individual freedom.

Between these extremes lies Europe, which is much less culturally monolithic than many non-Europeans realize. In northern Europe and Scandinavia, the patriarchal family structure has long been undergoing a radical transformation. This same development is just now beginning to gather impetus in southern Europe, even though the Catholic Church, in particular, is fighting to maintain masculine supremacy and to secure the obedience of women and children. (Viewed from a family therapeutic perspective, the patriarchal family structure of the south is often merely a social and economic reality. Psychologically and existentially, the apparently male-dominated families often prove to be matriarchies in disguise.)

This kaleidoscope of changing values, and the periodic absence of values, presents modern parents with a long (and essentially personal) list of choices that would not even have been thinkable for their own grandparents. How is it then possible to make everyday decisions, both great and small, when none of us can agree on what "should" be done? Should one seek out new authorities or trust one's own intuition and experience? Should one have faith in the humanitarian values that this world so clearly lacks, or should one concentrate solely on one's own material well being?

The choice is difficult—so difficult that many parents manage only to drift along on the current. Yet the terms are clearly drawn. Do we want to bring up our children so that they learn to rely on a solid internal authority, which will enable them to make their own social and existential choices? This is the approach many Scandinavian parents are beginning to adopt. Or do we want to teach them to place all their trust in an external authority, whether political, religious, or philosophical? To answer this question, let's look at an example that illustrates the limits—and significance—of a parent's responsibility.

Parental Responsibility and Power

Example: Three-year-old Jacob is shopping with his father at the local mall. At first, Jacob holds his father's hand, but when he becomes bored, he lets go and walks off to explore the stores on his own. His father runs after him, grabs his hand again, and says, "Jacob, you must stay with me and hold my hand. Remember that!"

Jacob protests and tries to wrench his hand out of his father's, but his father holds on tight. (Clearly, Jacob's father used his power and assumed parental responsibility; most parents would think that he has done the right thing.)

On their way out of the mall, they pass an ice-cream stand, and Jacob asks, "Dad, can I have a cone?"

His father says, "Not today, Jacob."

Jacob says, "Oh, Dad! I really want one. Why can't I have one?"

"Because I say so, Jacob . . . and because I'm the one who makes the decisions!"

Jacob asks again, but with the same result. Finally, he gives up and hangs his head as they walk out into the parking lot. (Again, most people would agree with Jacob's father's use of power.)

When they arrive home from their shopping trip, Jacob's father says, "Jacob, now it's time for you to have your afternoon nap!"

Jacob protests: he wants to play. But his father insists, explaining to Jacob that he will be too tired later on in the day if he does not sleep now. Jacob is tucked into bed and after tossing and turning for a quarter of an hour, he finally falls asleep. (Jacob's father has again used his power and assumed his parental responsibility, and most parents would agree that he has done the right thing.)

I agree with the majority of parents about the first two episodes—but not about the last one. In the first situation, there is no question that Jacob is too young to explore the mall on his own. What's at issue isn't jacob's biological and intellectual limitations—if he were living on the streets of Bombay or Prague, he would have had no trouble whatsoever navigating the city alone—but rather our societal values. In our culture, it is not good or safe for a three-year-old to be left on his own, and it is the responsibility of the parents to make sure that it does not happen.

In order to live up to this responsibility, Jacob's father was obliged to use a minimum of physical force. His verbal instruction to Jacob was also appropriate. It did not insult Jacob or injure his dignity. In the second episode, Jacob's father exercised his economic power, again, without insulting his son verbally.

The third episode, however, is more complex. In the first example, Jacob needed a guide in relation to the world around him. But the need for sleep is a very personal, biological need, about which his father can only have an educated opinion (unless Jacob's father is couching his own need for some peace and quiet as a need for Jacob to have a rest). Even though his opinion may happen to be correct for that particular Saturday afternoon, he can achieve only one goal: that Jacob sleeps for an hour—a short-term result.

But perhaps this is the way in which Jacob's father understands his parental responsibility—that he has to tell his son what his needs are and make sure that they are fulfilled, so that Jacob can learn what is best for him. (Jacob's father will also take responsibility for fulfilling a number of Jacob's other needs, which I will return to later.) Let's consider some of the consequences of his assuming responsibility in this way. First of all, Jacob's need for sleep will remain externally controlled. This may be pleasant enough for his parents as long as he is a young child. But imagine Jacob as a young teenager asking his parents if it's time for him to go to bed. Inevitably, they will become irritated with him and say, "You must be old enough to figure that out for yourself!" Jacob will then feel angry and confused; after all, he has spent thirteen years learning to sleep when his parents thought that he needed to. In other words, he has made an effort to cooperate and wishes to do the "right" thing. Now that he is demonstrating his compliance, they inform him that he is "wrong" and should be more independent.

Second, Jacob and his parents will have many conflicts as he grows up. At the very least, he will begin to "pester" them for permission to stay up late, and his parents will either refuse or give in, more or less as the wind blows; or they will make a number of set rules ("Then there is nothing to discuss!"). In many families, the situation is worse. Conflicts at bedtime erupt on a daily basis. Now suppose that

Jacob has a little sister who insists on going to bed at the same time that he does. You can see how unpleasant this would be.

Conflicts of this kind are not just exhausting for both parties. They also convey to Jacob that he is an inconvenience for his parents when he attempts to be true to himself, and thereby he learns a principle that will be destructive for him in every subsequent loving relationship: "In order to be loved, you must betray yourself!"

Some children cope with this principle by becoming defiant. If defiance develops into a personality trait, these children end up rejecting both the demands of other people and their own needs. Survival becomes a question of pointedly not doing what other people think one should do. **Defiance, though, is not a natural attitude; it is a survival strategy that children develop only when their self-esteem is threatened within the family.**

What is the alternative? What can Jacob's father do if he thinks that his son really needs an afternoon nap? He can simply say so to Jacob: "Jacob, listen. I think you need an hour's sleep. What do you think?"

Jacob will probably answer in one of the following ways:

- "Not just now. I want to play first."

- "I'm not sleepy today."

- "No! I want to play with my cars!"

To which his father may reply:

- "O.K., just play till you feel sleepy."

- "I think you are sleepy, but of course you only need to take a nap if you feel sleepy."

- "Yes, I can see you've lined them up ready to play with. I know what I need. I need to sit quietly for half an hour and read my newspaper."

And what if Jacob becomes grumpy and difficult toward the end of the afternoon? Then his father can say, "It's not much fun being with you when you're like this, Jacob. Maybe you should have had that nap after all."

In this scenario, parents have to put up with the inconvenience of having a difficult child around for a much shorter time than if they had continued to assume responsibility for the child's sleep. Not only is the unpleasant interval of time shorter, but it is also less destructive for both parties than if the conflict over sleep had been allowed to escalate. Those parents who put this principle into practice when their children are babies know the pleasure of having a child who, at the age of eighteen months or two years, says on his own initiative, "I want to sleep." Some days this child will get the sleep he needs, and other days he will not sleep enough—exactly like his parents.

But more important: he will be actively involved in the process of developing his self-esteem and self-responsibility. Furthermore, when he becomes an adult he will be able to start his own family knowing that the personal needs of other people do not exist in order to offend me, and I am not wrong just because my needs are different from what other people assume them to be. It is accept-able to express your needs and to be wrong, now and then.

On another level, the exchange between Jacob and his father is more than just the solution to an acute conflict. It is also a practical example of a mutual learning process. When Jacob's father says, "I need half an hour to read the paper," he is discovering his own limits and thereby exercising his sense of personal responsibility. He may miss this opportunity if he merely exercises his power by saying, "You must have an afternoon nap because you're tired, and that's that!"—or if he makes rules, saying, "You know very well that you have to have an afternoon nap every day!"

If his dad exerts his power, Jacob learns only either to submit to it or to resist it. If his father refrains from using power in this instance, he provides his son and himself with a unique opportunity to see how valuable they are to each other, and how they can help each other evolve. At the same time, Jacob will have the chance to

- see his father as a role model—someone who teaches him how adults express and negotiate their own needs and assume responsibility for themselves and their family;

- become fluent in personal language (which I will explain later in this chapter);

- develop his own sense of personal responsibility.

Children's Personal Responsibility

There are three areas of their lives for which children must be allowed to assume responsibility in order to stay healthy

- Their senses, for example, what tastes good and what does not, what smells pleasant or unpleasant, what feels cold, hot, and so forth.

- Their feelings, for example, happiness, love, friendship, anger, frustration, sorrow, pain, desire, and so forth, and in relation to whom and what.

- Their needs, for example, hunger, thirst, sleep, nearness, distance.

Later in life they will be responsible for the interests they pursue in their spare time, their education, their choice of clothing and appearance, and their religious practice.

What does it mean that children should assume responsibility for these areas of their physical, emotional, and intellectual existence? Does it mean that they should always make the decisions? That they should always have their own way? That they should always do just as they please?

In order to answer this I must take a linquistic turn: To *decide* has to do with power whereas to be *responsible for* something has to do with responsibility. The two phenomenon overlap to a certain degree but they are very different.

These questions will inevitably arise as long as the majority of adults still come from families whose philosophies of child rearing are based on old values. In these parents' minds, the concept of according children equal dignity will be construed as granting them "freedom"—which is diametrically opposed to the "constraint" that these parents experienced while they were growing up. Such parents regard the parent-child relationship as a power struggle. Every issue is boiled down to one essential consideration: who makes the decisions and who is going to hold sway. The terms of the struggle for power—whether it is fought exclusively on those conditions decided by the adults, or on more democratic principles—is not important in this connection because the struggle is, fundamentally, a fight for power. Returning to Jacob's situation, it is not really a question of Jacob's desire to play or his father's need to rest, but of the power struggle between them. Yet these struggles lead to a blind alley in which none of the parties gets what he or she needs.

If we really want to safeguard the integrity of parents and children, and to help children develop a healthy sense of self-esteem and of personal and social responsibility (these three concepts— integrity, self-esteem, and responsibility—are inseparable), then a new concept must be introduced into the family. **We need to take ourselves and our children seriously instead of clinging to an outdated conception of how to distribute power.**

This idea sounds deceptively easy. It is not the same as "allowing" somebody to do something. If Jacob asks if he can play with his cars and his father says, "Yes," then Jacob's father has allowed him to do so. When we talk about taking another person seriously, words are not enough in themselves. Often we need to hear "the sound" of the words or the tone of voice in order to determine whether a person is being taken seriously or whether she is being patronized.

To take another person seriously necessitates that we

- Acknowledge the other person's right to have the needs, desires, experiences, feelings, and right to expression that she actually has;

- See the other person's need from her point of view;

- concentrate on the other person so that we can get to know her reality without undermining her or her aspirations;

- reply to her actions with understanding and while also taking our own position seriously.

Example: Let's picture a long line at the checkout counter of a department store. A four-year-old girl goes up to her mother, who is last in line, pulls on her mother's arm, and says in a desperate voice, choking back tears, "Mom! I don't want to stay here any longer. Why can't we go home? I don't want to be here anymore!"

How would a mother reply? If she came from an old-fashioned family, she would feel compelled to give her daughter social instructions about how to behave, such as: "No, you must be quiet. When you go into stores, you must wait nicely until it's your turn."

A more contemporary mom from a democratic family would have appealed to her daughter's understanding by supplying both an objective observation and a diversionary tactic: "No, that's not possible. I understand that you're tired, but you can see that there are a lot of people waiting ahead of me. Have you seen those lovely dresses hanging over there?"

Neither of these comments is "wrong," nor did either mother violate her child's integrity in a direct way. Indirectly, however, in both instances the child was given the message that her feelings and needs are not as important as her mother's. The first mother ignores her child's feelings and needs; the second offers distraction as compensation. In both cases, the child is urged to take her parent's way of experiencing reality seriously, without the parent having to reciprocate.

Now let's study two mothers' different reactions to the same situation.

When Ruth's daughter pulls at her sleeve, Ruth pulls herself away from her daughter's grip, grabs hold of the girl's upper arm, and says aggressively, "Now stop that! You stay right here until we're finished! Do you understand!?"

Just as the girl looks as if she is going to answer, her mother attempts to lift her up into the stroller. But the girl falls onto the floor where she lies inert, chanting, "No, no, I want to go. Don't make me stay." With difficulty and suppressed anger, the mother manages to lift the child up, but the girl is so rigid that it is impossible to put her into the stroller. The mother becomes desperate and says in a hissing undertone, "That's enough now, you stupid girl. Sit down, or else."

At that second, the girl's crying changes from frustrated, choked protest to deep sobbing, and her body becomes completely limp, so that her mother can put her in the stroller without difficulty. The girl continues sobbing quietly until her mother has paid and they leave the store.

Lena and her four-year-old daughter are also stuck waiting in a long line. This girl, however, approaches her mother by saying, "Mom, it's not nice here now. . . . Can't we go home soon?"

In response, Lena says, in a kind voice, "You're right. It really is terribly hot in here, and look at all these people! I've just got to pay for this before we go. Couldn't you and your sister hang up those socks over there?" she asks, pointing to a pile of children's socks that have fallen off a rack.

The girl fetches her little sister and together they hang up the socks. When they have finished, they come back to their mother. The younger girl sits down in the stroller, while her sister asks for her pacifier.

What's the major difference between these two mothers? Lena takes her daughter seriously; Ruth does not.

Ruth's daughter addresses her mother in a language and tone of voice that reveal that she is not used to being taken seriously. From her first words, she is defensive and complaining, and from a superficial perspective, her tone tends to make her sound self-centered and irritating. But what this really means is that by the young age of four the girl has already learned that her desires and needs are either unimportant or annoying to her mother, or both. The girl persists in struggling for the right to feel of value, but loses more often than she wins. Ruth's response in the store once again confirms the girl's experience.

But Ruth herself is not used to being taken seriously, and she is therefore unable to see her daughter's needs as anything other than annoying in relation to her own. The result is a struggle for power, in which the girl's integrity is violated both physically and mentally. It is true that the mother appears to win the struggle for power, but in fact both of them lose in the sense that neither of them gets what she wants. The daughter loses a little bit more of her self-esteem and her trust in other people; the mother experiences yet again her own low self-esteem and loses a bit more of her maternal self-confidence. In addition, their relationship deteriorates.

Only time will tell whether Ruth's daughter will become so broken that she will turn sweet and docile, or whether she will begin to violate her mother with the same kind of desperate brutality that her mother has visited on her. If this incident had taken place thirty or forty years ago, the child would have been forced to adapt. The destructive element in her childhood would not have taken its toll on her psychological well-being until she became an adult. Today, the results often manifest themselves more quickly. By the time she reaches puberty, she will probably begin to engage in self-destructive behavior.

Now let's return to Lena. The way in which Lena's daughter approaches her mother reveals that she comes from a family where it is acceptable to express one's desires and needs, and where one can count on being taken seriously. Lena's response confirms this. She is aware that her daughter wants to cooperate and likes to feel valuable. She therefore solves their mutual dilemma by asking the girl to do something useful while they wait. The daughter does not get what she really wants, but she does receive confirmation of her feelings. Even though her needs conflict with her mother's, she is learning to trust her mother. Furthermore, she is able to assume responsibility for her own well-being during the time they are forced to wait.

The question of who is a better mother is of little interest. Both mothers do the best they can in this situation according to what they have learned, and it is meaningless to grade them. What's important about these scenarios is that Ruth's relationship to her daughter is painful for both of them—and that there is a way out of this pain, which can be learned.

Neither of the two girls got what they wanted—neither of them was "allowed" to do what she wanted to do or to get her "way"— but only Lena took both her daughter's and her own needs seriously, acknowledged their needs as being of equal value, and assumed the overriding parental responsibility so that the integrity of neither of them was violated.

What distinguishes Lena from mothers of earlier generations is that she demonstrates both personal and social responsibility instead of teaching her daughter about it. She becomes a model with whom her daughter can cooperate, instead of being an authority who teaches something that she herself does not practice. She knows that it is not a question of either/or (that is, either I do what you want to do, or you do what I want to do). Her daughter learns, without being instructed, that it is necessary to wait when you stand in line. She also learns that her mother takes her needs seriously.

The experience of being taken seriously is not a concrete experience but a "musical" one, and therefore children have difficulty explaining to themselves when that is what they lack in their family. When eloquent children with flexible parents attempt to put it into words, they will often express it like this: "My Mom and Dad decide everything. I'm never allowed to decide anything." Both statements are often objectively wrong, but that's because very few children can express their experience of not being taken seriously by their parents. Instead, they report that they feel left out of the decision process.

Less eloquent children from less flexible families are forced to revert to symptomatic behavior: they become highly opinionated, demanding, overscrupulous, or power hungry and bossy. But adults have difficulty interpreting the meaning of these behaviors, so the underlying problem—that the children feel as if they are not being taken seriously—remains unaddressed. What these children need is a personal language with which to express their core feelings.

A Personal Language

All of us are multilingual. As children, we learn several different languages (apart from foreign languages):

- social language, which is used in ordinary social situations in which politeness and some degree of indirection are necessary

- academic language, which is used to describe and analyze scientific problems

- literary language, which is used when we write

None of these three languages is suitable for expressing, dealing with, or solving interpersonal conflicts. If we "talk" or "chat" about conflicts in our social language, we may feel relieved but we won't reach a resolution. Psychology, with its academic professional jargon, can analyze and describe our conflicts and problems, but it cannot solve them. Some authors can apparently "write themselves out of their problems," but it is not the words and sentences in their books that set them free. Rather these are literary testaments to the healing process.

In order to assume responsibility for ourselves in relation to other people, without cutting off or complicating the contact we have with them, we need to have a personal language. By this I mean a language with which we can express our feelings, reactions, and needs and set our limits. This personal language is the first language children begin to speak, irrespective of whether their parents have a personal language.

The nucleus of a personal language is

I want to. I don't want to.

I like. I don't like.

I will. I will not.

(Personal language must not be confused with the type of quasi-personal language that has evolved in the past twenty-five years, which is psychological in origin and is based on the notion that people need to "talk about their feelings." Using this language, it is possible, to a certain extent, to describe oneself to others, but this language lacks the liberating and contact intensifying power of personal language. Statements starting with the expression "I feel . . .," for example, rarely take on the same personal intensity as saying "I want . . ."). Talking about our feelings might have a certain social value but for our mental health as well as for the quality of our relationships with people we love and care about the ability to *express* ourselves verbally and emotionally is far more important.

The personal language of children is initially more immediate and "raw" than that of adults. It gives a precise picture of the child's existence at that precise moment. In autocratic families, personal language is forbidden; parents in these families go to great lengths to ensure that their children learn to "speak properly" and discharge their personal language. But in families that prize treating each member with equal dignity, children must develop their own personal language, and parents and other adults must help them do so.

Here are three brief exchanges. In each dialogue one parent respects his child's personal language and one doesn't:

Child: I don't want to go to bed now.

Respectful Dad: I want you to go to bed now.

Disrespectful Dad: Now be a good boy, and do as I say.

Or: Now that's enough! You go to bed when you're told to, and that's final!

Child: I don't like onion.

Respectful Dad: Aha! I like onion. I think you ought to try it.

Disrespectful Dad: Now don't be silly! You usually like onion.

Or: Now don't you be so fussy! You eat what's on your plate just like the rest of us.

Child: I want to play with your computer.

Respectful Dad: I don't want you to play with my computer.

Disrespectful Dad: Why do you always have to be so irritating?

When personal language is allowed to develop in an atmosphere in which it is respected, children's integrity is not violated, and they learn to set their own limits without violating the boundaries of other people. At the same time, in the process of teaching children to become fluent in their personal language, both parents and children learn who they are. In contrast, the more traditional approach is for parents to tell children who they should be or become. Ironically, this approach serves to make parents more anxious about whom their children really are.

Personal language – growing and developing simultaneously with self-esteem – is the only way to increased personal responsibility which again is the only road to mental and social health.

Luckily it's not completely up to parents and the rest of us adults. More and more children and young people are discovering the value of personal responsibility and are simply taking it. They are very aware that this is considered dangerous among adults and they express this awareness in beautifull, creative slogans like: I'm your future! Are you scared? Not only are they pinpointing the growing fear of youth they are also exposing the hollowness of old platitudes like: our children are our future!

Responsible, But Not Alone

Children are able to indicate the scope of their personal responsibility and integrity from birth by using noises and gestures:

- Babies who aren't hungry turn their heads away from their mother's breast or regurgitate.

- When babies are too cold or too hot, or if they are wet, they inform adults by fussing or crying.

- Young children naturally approach people they are attracted to and reject those they feel repelled by.

- Young children choose clothes that reflect their mood rather than those that suit the weather.

To my way of thinking, this indicates that babies and young children are very competent in terms of communicating their limits and what they want and need; still, they often need adult help translating their hints into clear, understandable statements. In addition, although children are able to express their needs and boundaries, they remain unable to defend them against manipulation and infringements from older children or adults. They therefore depend on the ability and willingness of their adult caretakers to recognize their competencies and their right to exercise their personal responsibility. But these adults need to be both trustworthy—that is, true to themselves— and open—that is, prepared to acknowledge that people experience reality in different ways.

Consider, for example, the following exchanges between a child and a respectful and a disrespectful parent.

Child: Daddy, I'm freezing!

Respectful Dad: Are you? I'm just fine. . . . Well, let's see about getting you something else to put on.

Disrespectful Dad: Don't be silly. It's not cold at all. just look at me. I've only got a T-shirt on like you.

Child: Mom, I don't like my new English teacher.

Respectful Mom: Oh . . . that surprises me. She seems nice to me. . . . What is it you don't like about her?

Disrespectful Mom: What's the matter now? I suppose she's insisting that you hand in your work on time.

Child: Mom, you know the party on Saturday . . . ? I thought about wearing the green shirt. Do you think I could wear that?

Respectful Mom: You look nice in the green one, but I prefer you in the white one.

Disrespectful Mom: Don't you think you're getting carried away with all this dressing up? You have so many nice clothes that it doesn't really matter what you put on.

All the inappropriate adult replies have two things in common: they discount the child's competence, and they attempt to "educate." In effect, these comments say, "You should not feel and experience things the way you do. It would be better for you to feel and experience as I do."

But what about the educational dimension? Perhaps the mother of the boy who doesn't like his English teacher is seriously concerned about the fact that her son ought to be able to appreciate competent teachers when he meets them, or perhaps she thinks that he takes his schoolwork too lightly. Surely these are legitimate, important concerns. Perhaps the mother in the third example is worried that her daughter has started to spend too much time dolling herself up. This is equally legitimate.

But, when expressed in this way, both the concerns themselves and the timing are problematic. If parents have important issues to discuss with their children, they need to choose a time and place for that particular conversation so that they have the opportunity to say everything that is on their mind. This is a way of taking themselves seriously. If they try to take a shortcut, they will neither make an impression nor be taken seriously. In other words, disrespectful comments do not have the educative effect that parents desire and/ or the child might need.

Such efforts also backfire because disrespectful responses make children feel wrong or stupid. As a result, children disregard the lesson the parents are so intent on imparting. According to every educational theory, people who consider themselves to be stupid or wrong do not learn anything.

Example: To illustrate what I mean, let me introduce Lily, sixteen, and her boyfriend Frank, eighteen, who have known each other for several months. One day Lily comes home from school and says, "Mom, Frank and I wondered whether you and Dad would think it was all right if I spent the night at his place this weekend."

Assuming that Lily lives in a society in which such a question is reasonable, how should her mother respond? Her mom is aware of what her daughter wants to do, but she is not sure if her daughter knows what she needs. Lily is not asking to stay over at her boyfriend's house because she wants to make love with him; she can do that at other times and places without her parents' permission. She asks for two reasons: she wants to make love with her boyfriend and wants her parents to know that she is doing so, and she needs to know what her mother thinks and feels about the idea. She wants to tell her mother who she is now, and she wants to know what her mother thinks about the person she is now. In other words, Lily does not need lectures instructing her about sex and contraception, or lessons about AIDS or morality. She needs feedback that is just as open and personal as her own approach (provided that the aim is to strengthen the development of her self-esteem and personal responsibility, and preserve and deepen the contact between herself and her mother).

Lily's mother might respond like this:

"Phew! Right now, I just don't know what to say to you. I really feel like saying, 'NO, NO, NO!' I know that you're sixteen, but in my heart you're still only about ten. . . . Couldn't you wait fifteen or twenty years, for my sake?. . . . . . Of course, I don't really mean that, but just now when you asked me, I didn't really know what to answer. Can you give me a chance to think about it and talk to your father first? Then I'll be able to tell you what I think."

This response does not give Lily a direct answer to her question, but she has been given something much better: an open, honest, and very personal reaction from her mother. And initially, that is what the teenager needs most. In this way, contact between mother and daughter has been established. If at some future time Lily should need information and guidance, or if she should find herself in a moral dilemma, the door of communication between her and her mother is open.

Or, her mother could say:

"I don't think you should! I've noticed how fond you are of Frank, so I was prepared that you might ask me something like this. It's not up to me to decide whom you go out with, but I have to tell you that in my eyes Frank is not the boy I would like to see you with. I'm not saying this to forbid you, but you asked for my opinion and that's the way I feel."

This response has the same qualities (minus the humor) as the first one. Presumably, Lily would have preferred it if her mother had been pleased about her relationship with Frank, but that is not often the case. This reaction, though, is much better for Lily, her mother, and their mutual relationship than some kind of vague, nonconfrontational answer, such as: "Oh, I really don't know, Lily. You are fond of Frank. . . . That's up to you to decide. . . . What do you think?" (The question of giving teenagers permission or forbidding them to do things will be considered in Chapter 7.)

Personal feedback is the only form of communication that accomplishes three things at once: it develops children's personal responsibility in a discriminating way; it maintains and develops children's relationships with their parents; and it promotes feelings of family unity. All other forms of feedback—factual, moral, and social instruction; value judgments; and indifference—are destructive when it comes to promoting the three beneficial conditions just described. The latter forms of feedback cause children to become externally rather than internally controlled (which is in turn detrimental to both their self-esteem and their development of personal responsibility), and lead to feelings of isolation, inferiority, or shame. All of which are well known preconditions for self-destructive behavior.

Furthermore, using personal feedback has an added advantage. It constantly reminds children and young people of the existence of other people, other attitudes, and other ways of experiencing reality. In this important way, it helps to develop their social awareness and responsibility.

For adults, choosing to work toward achieving a more equally dignified relationship with children and young people is a daily challenge. Every day, children try to define their personal limits and personal responsibility. In response, parents need to dig slightly deeper and come up with new ways of responding, rather than resorting to the same old standard reactions. To do so, parents need to shift their consciousness toward a more authentic way of being. They have to give up saying things like, "That's not what we usually do," "Everybody else says that . . . " or "In our family we have always . . ."

In other words, parents have to abandon "the automatic parental answering machine," the device that spouts educative, advisory, and "helpful" comments as soon as a child gets within earshot. Of course, the truth about the automatic parental answering machine is that the great majority of children stop listening to its messages by the time they are five, and most adults immediately forget what they themselves have programmed it to say. But this is understandable because the quality of the messages is, to put it kindly, unreliable. Most often, the tape contains an unsorted hodgepodge of "received wisdom" we remember from our grandparents, along with various bits and pieces of more contemporary parental advice we read in a magazine or overheard on television.

But just because the tape is automatic doesn't mean that it's harmless. Far from it. The individual words may sound harmless enough, but the underlying message is destructive: "You would not be able to function as a decent/well-bred/ responsible/cooperative child unless I remind you all the time what you should do!" Or as my parents expressed it, "You ought to be glad that you have us! What would become of you otherwise?" And the more often the tape repeats itself, the more clearly the message is registered in the minds of children who trust their parents so much and so deeply that they integrate the underlying message and ultimately consider themselves to be wrong, bad or naughty. Even when the reach the age of fourty.

Children's ability to express and practice their self-responsibility increases with age. The same can apply to adult self-responsibility—but best if adults are open to acknowledging their own competencies and those of their children.

Responsibility Versus Service

Not all that many years ago, children were expected to carry out a number of service functions within the family. For example, children were expected to do their "chores" as a token of gratitude for the love and upbringing they received from their parents. When children balked at or did not embrace the chores assigned them, parents would often say, "They treat their home as if it was a boardinghouse."

Over the last fifteen to twenty years, I've become aware of a group of parents who do the opposite: instead of asking their children to perform appropriate chores, they wait on their children. This approach appears loving and caring, as long as the children are young and the exchange is harmonious. But when children reach the age of three and four, tensions often erupt. As children's demands become more unreasonable and absurd, parents become more frustrated. In the worst examples, parents end up permanently resentful and exhausted, and their children develop into asocial beings, unbearable to live with.

Professionals have labeled these children with various "diagnoses" such as "The New Child Character" and "The Little Tyrants." Several years passed before professionals began to focus attention on the parents, asking how and why they behaved the way they did. I have always found it very interesting to work with the parents of such children, and I have had the opportunity to do so in various

European countries. They represent a vanguard in the evolution of relationships between parents and children.

These typically "modern" parents are often very aware of their relationship with their children. They have approached child rearing with a great deal of thought and have generally rejected the tyrannical parent role of earlier generations, consciously distancing themselves from the way in which they were brought up. They remember all too well how frustrated and degraded they felt as children when their own parents made decisions for them. These recollections are now imprinted in their consciousness as a sense of never having been able to have or do what they wanted. (This phenomenon can also be observed in families in which the parents have not thought things through so clearly but feel perpetually uncertain and powerless.)

Suppose, for example, that as a child Henry had to eat hot cereal for breakfast even though he didn't like it, and then he was criticized for being hungry between meals. Suppose that Lisa always had to clean her plate even when she was full. Suppose that Mark, who always wanted new toys, was constantly criticized by his parents who told him, "You can't always get everything you ask for! 'I want this, I want that.' You always want something! My dear child, do you ever think about the fact that there has to be room for the rest of us? Anyway, you've just had your birthday, and soon it will be Christmas. You should understand that we have to save money now and then! "I'm not interested in what you 'want.' "I want you to say, 'I would like or please.' "

Naturally enough, when Henry and Lisa and Mark become parents, they may conclude that they must give their children what they want, whenever possible. In this way, they not only avoid making the mistake their own parents made, but they also see their gesture as an obvious expression of love and care, even though it has neither a loving nor a caring effect. This approach, like so many other actions taken in child rearing, is just lovingly meant.

Essentially, the question of personal responsibility has gone awry in these families. As I mentioned before, children know what they want, but they don't know what they need. If parents try to give children what they want, then children simply do not get what they need which is experienced, informed parental leadership. Instead, they become neglected. In addition, when the good feeling in a family is based on providing children with everything they want, parents teach children to equate love and care with getting what they want. Consequently, children step up their demands for service. And the more their demands escalate, the more pain they feel because of their neglect, and the more they demand as compensation. In other words, they cooperate with the philosophy of their parents.

What's lacking in these families is a dialogue between children and parents. In their eagerness to be caring and nonauthoritarian, these parents overlook their own needs and their own integrity. As a result, their children never encounter personal opposition. Instead of tangling with flesh-and-blood parents, children receive a yes or a no and interpret the response in terms of whether or not their request for services will be met. In the long run, there can be no personal closeness without personal responsibility.

Adults can recognize this phenomenon in their own loving relationships. We all enjoy being waited on at times, especially if we take turns. But if your partner continually seeks out your needs, feelings, and moods without ever revealing his own, you end up feeling very alone and frustrated! It's difficult enough for an adult to approach her partner and say, "Listen, I know that you want to give me everything that I desire, but I never get what I need most of all: YOU!"

Children would find it impossible to articulate this experience. Instead, they reach an inevitable and painful conclusion: "When my parents give me everything I ask for and I still feel that I am lacking something, then there must be something wrong with me." And their parents inevitably come to the same conclusion: "We give our children everything that we are capable of giving them, and still something is missing. We must be bad parents!" This is one of the most explosive and destructive types of parent-child relationships. Both parties rapidly lose their self-esteem and self-confidence, and at the same time they develop feelings of aggression and guilt.

There is only one way out. The solution is both simple and difficult at the same time, and it begins with two decisive steps.

First, parents must assume full responsibility for the fact that family interactions have developed in such a destructive way. They must sit down together with their children and say, "We are sorry that you are feeling bad about how things are going. We also feel bad about it. We want to tell you that it is our fault. We always thought that we were doing the very best for you when we gave you what you wanted, but now we realize that we have been wrong. We were so eager to make you happy and satisfied that we forgot ourselves. Now, things are going to change. It won't be easy for any of us, but we think that we can get through this. Of course, we would be pleased if you would cooperate with us so that we can make our family a happier one."

The next step takes considerably longer. It requires that parents make a serious attempt to find "themselves"—their own limits, desires, feelings, values and needs. They also need to practice expressing themselves as "purely" as possible, which is, without criticizing their children or appealing for their understanding or their one-sided cooperation. As a general rule, children are able to cooperate with the new approach after parents embrace and practice it. Their responsibility can develop only in tandem with their parents', although at a somewhat slower pace.

How can parents train themselves to reveal their own feelings, needs, and limits? Not by staging long, profound conversations with their children, but by remembering to "include themselves" in simple, everyday exchanges. Parents need to use personal language.

Example: Instead of saying, "I finish work early today. What would you prefer: shall I pick you up at your friend's house at three o'clock, or will you come home on your own at five?"

Say, "I finish work early today and I'd like to pick you up at three o'clock. What do you think?"

Instead of asking, "What would you like for dinner?" Say, "I'd like fish for dinner today. What would you like?"

Instead of asking, "Wouldn't you like to go to bed early this evening?"

Say, "I'd like a few hours to myself this evening. What would you say about going to bed early?"

Instead of saying, "We're free this weekend. What would you like to do?"

Say, "We're free this weekend, and we thought about just staying at home and relaxing. What do you think we should do?"

Instead of saying, "It's rather cold today. Don't you think you should put some warmer clothes on?"

Say, "It's cold today, so I'd like you to put some warm clothes on."

Instead of asking, "Wouldn't you like to help your dad in the garden this afternoon?"

Say, "I'd like you to help Dad in the garden this afternoon."

The difference between these approaches may seem slight and perhaps even superficial if you focus on the words and the tactical phrasing. But the real difference lies in the quality of the responses: the initial statements create feelings of loneliness within families, while the rephrasings create feelings of togetherness. When parents begin speaking in the way I recommend, children begin to experience their parents in an authentic way—that is, children experience their parents as "real." Only then can their social responsibility begin to develop.

When parents first begin to speak in a personal language, conflicts with their children may well increase rather than subside. This behavior is an understandable backlash. In turn, parents may be tempted to revive some remedies from the past—"setting limits," "being consistent," and "establishing consequences." These methods can work for a limited period of time if parents are persistent and staunch in their efforts, but they are a very shortsighted solution, and there are many good reasons to caution against this approach.

In the most positive light, such a retreat will reduce the number of conflicts—but only on the surface. Rather than arguing with each other, family members will begin to experience conflicts within themselves (intrapsychic conflicts), which unavoidably reappear as interpersonal conflicts. This happens for two reasons: First, the old-fashioned methods ultimately put all the responsibility and blame on the children. Second, these approaches only appear to fill the vacuum, but they don't: the lack of closeness between adults and children remains. Children still do not receive what they need. At the most, they learn to behave as if they did. By the same token, parents do not grow as adults. They just erect a "child-rearing plan" between themselves and their children. The contact between them may change, but it won't improve.

Similar issues apply to families with children who are diagnosed with Attention Deficit Disorder (ADD), which is assumed to account for their highly impulsive and asocial behavior. It is vital that the parents of these children learn how to demonstrate their limits and feelings to their children without relying on a "method." Otherwise, the children's quality of life will be impaired in the long run—and their symptoms will grow worse. Just as important, their parents will feel used up. The fact that these children are given a diagnosis often helps to relieve their parents' feelings of guilt— and that is important—but resorting to a "child-rearing approach" will damage the parents' self-esteem as well as their relationship to their children. Children, irrespective of personality or diagnosis, do not benefit from being subjected to pedagogical methods unless the purpose is to teach them intellectual or practical skills.

CHILDREN'S SOCIAL
RESPONSIBILITY

I firmly believe that having a sense of social responsibility enhances the quality of human life. We are all connected, for better or worse, and any notion that we can avoid influencing the lives of other people and being influenced by theirs is an illusion. The same principle applies to societies and families: there is no such thing as your problem and my problem. It is a question of our problem and our success.

As I mentioned, it is my experience that children who are given support to develop their self-responsibility almost automatically develop a high degree of social responsibility. These children are helpful, sensitive, and considerate—manifestations of their social responsibility. In this context, social responsibility is not expressed as self-sacrifice, but as conscious, joint responsibility, which to a much greater degree ensures the dignity of all parties concerned.

Three-and four-year-old children begin developing their sense of social responsibility by practicing it with their parents and siblings.

Different families have different attitudes, and the extent to which a family requires that children develop social responsibility varies greatly, depending on such factors as the number of siblings and the family's social status and financial standing. Some families promote social responsibility by stressing the importance of emotional expression in the form of consideration and flexibility, and other families cultivate practical helpfulness and a sense of duty in terms of thought and deed.

The extent to which children develop a sense of social responsibility also varies from country to country. Daycare centers and kindergartens in some countries emphasize the development of "freedom with responsibility"; others measure children's social responsibility on the basis of their capability and willingness to subject themselves to the rules of the institution. Despite these differences, there is one factor these institutions have in common: the more children believe that social responsibility derives from a *sense of duty*, the more likely it is that they will grow up to be adults whose sense of social responsibility is underdeveloped.

There are two basic prerequisites for the optimal development of children's social responsibility:

- that parents see and acknowledge children's urges to cooperate, and

- that parents behave responsibly toward each other, their children, and other people.

As I have already mentioned, adults who set an example through actions impress their children far more than those who simply give verbal instructions.

Example: Four-year-old Kevin is sitting on the floor playing with his Legos. His little sister walks by and stops for several minutes to watch her big brother with curiosity and admiration. Finally, she can no longer contain herself. She takes a few Legos so that she can play with him. Kevin tries to get her to stop without success, and finally he pushes her away. She bursts into a heartrending howl. Their mother is alarmed and comes running into the room.

Mother: What's happened? What's the matter?

Little sister (crying): Kevin hit me! Kevin: I didn't . . . she keeps touching my Legos.

Mother: Kevin, you know you mustn't hit your little sister. You have to remember that you are the oldest and that she is too young to understand. Why can't she help you build with Legos? Couldn't you play with your sister when you can see how much she wants to play with you!?

This is a classic example of a somewhat simplified understanding of social responsibility—"Those who are older must be good to the young"—and of an instructive upbringing. The mother's remarks are quite understandable. She cannot accept that Kevin violates his sister's personal limits every time the little girl, through childish folly, violates his. The problem is that the mother acts inconsiderately toward Kevin while at the same time instructing him to be considerate.

Here's an alternative dialogue:

Mother: What has happened, Kevin? Kevin: She keeps spoiling my Legos! Little sister: Kevin hit me, Mom! Mother (putting her arm around the little sister and keeping her attention on Kevin): Let's try to figure out what you can say to her when you want to play in peace.

In this version of the scenario, the mother does several important things at the same time:

- She investigates what has happened.

- She appeals to Kevin as the more responsible of the two children instead of instructing him about his responsibility.

- Her suggestion communicates that she is aware that Kevin has tried to set his own limits through the use of peaceful means, and that the situation culminated in a physical con-frontation only because he does not know any better.

- She acknowledges simultaneously his will to cooperate and his need to protect his own integrity.

- She takes care of Kevin's sister and at the same time allows the little girl to hear that Kevin's personal limits are important in the family.

- By not criticizing Kevin for using his physical superiority, his mother informs him that she is aware that he feels bad about the way the conflict developed.

- She indicates an approach instead of suggesting a solution. In this way she supports the development of Kevin's personal and social responsibility. At the same time she informs both her children that the art of safeguarding one's own integrity without causing injury to others is not something that you can "just do."

There is no need for the mother to continue the conversation beyond this point. Kevin's sense of responsibility will gradually lead him in the right direction.

Once respect for personal responsibility is established within the family, children are ready to be introduced to other types of social responsibility.

Practical Responsibility

During the 1950s and 1960s, the majority of professionals held the view that it was healthy for children to have chores—an unfortunate misperception. The principles from which this point of view springs are basically sound: children need to feel that they are a valuable part of the family. In the past, children were thought of as additional breadwinners. Now, in the more highly developed countries, they no longer need to fulfill this role. Hence, a vacuum has developed.

It is important, however, to draw a distinction between parents who ask children to do chores around the house because they need the help, and those who just think that work is "good" for kids. It may seem a small difference—and in reality, few parents may be aware that they are making a decision at all—but the distinction is enormous and has important consequences. Children who are asked to do chores because their parents need help experience themselves as valuable in relation to their parents, whereas those children whose parents feel that chores are "good" for children experience themselves as objects upon which theories of upbringing are being projected. Clearly, children in the latter category will have a hard time experiencing themselves as having value.

As I mentioned, families of different sizes differ in important ways. The larger the family, the greater the need for planning and structure, and thereby for duties. The question of assigning chores often arises when a child reaches five years of age. At this juncture, parents are faced with a very important decision: they can decide if they want to raise conscientious children or helpful children.

In actuality, the choice between raising helpful children or conscientious children is not necessarily an either/or question. But it is helpful to think of it in these terms for now in order to reflect on our long-term objectives for our children.

Parents who wish to have conscientious children need to take two basic factors into consideration:

- According to developmental psychologists, the healthiest activity for children younger than ten—in terms of their physical, mental, social, and intellectual development—is play.

- Eight-and nine-year-old children possess a limited perspective. They do not enter into contracts with the same awareness that adults do. For example, suppose you are washing up after dinner while your six-year-old daughter sits at the table chatting pleasantly with you. You ask if she'd like to wash the dishes three nights a week, and she says, eagerly, "Oh yes." But her yes does not mean, "I am prepared to wash up three times a week for as long as I live at home." It means, "Yes, I love you too, and right now I'm prepared to do anything at all to make you happy!" The alacrity with which your six-year-old enters into a "contract" with her mother is similar to one adult telling another, "I will always love you!"—which is neither a promise nor a contract, but an expression of how intensely one person feels about his love at that precise moment.

If we bear these two conditions in mind, there is nothing wrong with giving children a number of regular chores. But it is important that parents do not mix "love and business"; that parents do not adopt an approach that says, "You owe it to your parents to fulfill your duties as an expression of gratitude for their great love for you!"

Duties are duties; they have nothing to do with love. They may involve feelings of goodwill perhaps, and of responsibility, but not love. If a similar arrangement were drawn up between people who are married, their love would rapidly fade.

That's why it's important that children are given tasks that are meaningful for the family—for which their parents really need their help—and that children's efforts are appreciated.

Another advantage of giving children domestic chores is that doing so organizes their natural helpfulness and urge to cooperate. It helps the family, and it is in no way detrimental to children's development. At the same time, chores are not necessary; that is, taking on chores does not develop a child's sense of social responsibility. Parents need to decide whether to assign chores on the basis of their own needs and attitudes only.

If parents choose to have helpful children, they need to remember that helpfulness cannot be structured before the age of ten or eleven. Before this age, only a few children are able to cope with this kind of structure. Furthermore, it is important not to give them regular duties but instead to ask for their help whenever it is needed.

- "Simon! Remember that it's your turn to wash up today!" This parent is used to allotting chores.

- "Simon! I need some help. Will you wash up?" This parent is asking for help.

Since most children find themselves in the middle of doing something else when their parents request their help, parents shouldn't ask children if they "feel" like helping. Children never "feel" like stopping what they're engaged in at the moment. But parents can insist:

"Simon! I need some help. Will you do the dishes?" "No, I don't have time. I'm going to play football with Nicholas." "It's all right if you play football first, but I want you to do the dishes afterward, O.K.?"

Or:

"Simon! I want you to go down to the recycling bin with our old newspapers today. Would you do that?" "Oh no . . . I don't feel like it. I'm watching television." "That's all right, Simon! You don't have to feel like it. You can not feel like it all the way down there and back again, but I want those newspapers out of the house today!"

Or:

"Simon! I need your help for a moment. Would you set the table while I finish making the dinner?" "No! I'm busy!" "O.K. I'll do it myself."

And then, of course, there are all the occasions when children say, simply, "Yes." From my experience, there are two advantages when parents choose to raise helpful rather than conscientious children. In the long view, helpful children contribute more to the sense of family togetherness. Second, both parties receive essential training in saying yes and no to each other, and in that way they are sensitized to each other's needs and limits. It is important to frame the distinction not as a matter of choice versus duty, but as a question of whether one's sense of responsibility arises from within (intrinsic control) or from without (extrinsic control).

Like adults, children need to feel that they are of value to the family as a whole. Feeling valuable in this sense rarely—perhaps never— arises from the sense that one has performed a service. At the same time, children are deprived of feeling valued if they perceive that they are at their parents' beck and call, or if they feel as if they are the objects upon which their parents exercise their notions about how children "should" be raised. The purest form of conscientiousness—

that is, social responsibility that is not just governed by a sense of duty—emerges when both children and adults are free to commit themselves and not when they feel compelled to commit themselves in order to please other people.

Over-Responsible Children

We often become so involved in developing children's social responsibility on the practical level that we forget how responsible children feel, almost from birth, for their parents' well-being. Children feel guilty when their parents have personal or marital problems, or when parents treat them badly or neglect them. In these situations, children always come to the same emotional conclusion: that they are the ones in the wrong. Such children mature at an early age and are forced by circumstance to act as a parent for their own parent.

Some children become over-responsible at the young age of one or two. They learn to care for their parents' needs and repress their own. This is particularly apparent in families where one of the parents is a drug addict, an alcoholic, mentally ill, or emotionally absent.

But this situation also occurs in families whose circumstances are much less dramatic. For example, it applies to families in which a very young and immature girl has become a mother in an attempt to give her life meaning and coherence. It is not unusual in situations in which divorcing parents struggle for power, using the children as ammunition and claiming custody as a symbol of victory. (Unfortunately, this is an interpersonal process that no legislation can prevent.)

Children also may become over-responsible in divorced families in which one parent has been left in a critical situation characterized by feelings of hopelessness, bitterness, or paralyzing loneliness. Even if children live with this parent only part-time, they will sacrifice their own needs for the sake of the parent. Of course, some single parents abuse their children's responsibility and willingness to cooperate by shifting all their worries and cares onto their children's shoulders. Sadly, this problem is not restricted to single-parent families. It is just as relevant in two-parent families in which parents are unable to talk to each other about their problems, and where the mother, in particular, is driven to confide in a child. These children often very quickly develop a sense of over-responsibility, not just in relation to the mother's problems, but also with regard to their parents' matrimonial problems. Naturally this strain negatively affects the children's development.

Adult immaturity or existential emptiness is a vacuum that inevitably attracts children who need to be valued and wish to cooperate. From the parents' point of view, their relationship with their child appears satisfying and uncomplicated. But other adults in the child's life may see the problem—because a child compensates for the attention he doesn't receive from his parents by acting out with other adults. Younger children whine and cling; older children become aggressive and seek out conflicts. In this way, children ingeniously and competently seek to satisfy their own needs.

Thus far, I have described family situations that are quite clearly destructive, but it is important to point out that seemingly "normal" families raise over-responsible children as well. The following situation illustrates how difficult it is for parents to recognize the extent to which their own children cooperate.

Example: Andrew's parents divorced when he was three. Although his mother was somewhat bitter about the divorce, both parents took their responsibility toward their son very seriously: they didn't fight, and they continued to live near each other so that Andrew, spending alternate weeks with each parent, could maintain contact with his friends and stay at the same school.

Both parents were well educated. His mother, disenchanted with men in general, lived alone; his father chose to live alone, mostly out of consideration for Andrew, even though he had a couple of lengthy relationships with other women. After ten years, though, when Andrew turned thirteen, his father began living with a woman.

Andrew quickly established a good relationship with Hannah, his father's new partner. The apprehensions that the adults had concerning jealousy and conflicts proved to be unfounded.

Six months passed. One morning, Andrew's mother called on her ex-husband to say that Andrew had decided to stop visiting his father according to the arrangement they had worked out. This news came as a shock to the father. Feeling rejected and guilty, he considered several explanations: Was Andrew jealous after all? Was his former wife trying to spoil things? Did Andrew feel overlooked under the new circumstances?

Andrew and his parents ended up in therapy, and during a session, the father said, "Andrew, I would like to know why you suddenly don't want to live with me anymore? . . . I mean, as much as you used to."

Andrew hesitated and was quiet for a long time before speaking. Then, looking at his father with great seriousness, he said, "It's because I thought that now . . . now you have Hannah to look after you . . . perhaps you don't need me to come so often." The father was astounded, moved, and satisfied by the answer, and he was prepared to talk over a new arrangement with regard to Andrew's visits.

At this point Andrew's mother, who from the start of the meeting had insisted on her right to remain silent, interrupted by saying, "But Andrew, can you then explain why you suddenly want to go to boarding school?"

Once again, Andrew thought for a long time, but this time his courage let him down slightly. With encouragement from the family therapist, he managed to answer, "Then perhaps you might also find yourself a new husband."

These self-effacing, loving, and deeply responsible statements from a thirteen-year-old boy introduce us to the extent to which children cooperate with and feel responsible for their parents. And they serve as a good point from which to launch a discussion of the problems facing single parents—for in these families, the temptation to have a child step in and fill the parental void is hard to resist.

My experience indicates that most single parents are responsible, but that does not mean that they can always avoid raising over-responsible children. This is especially true if they became single parents before their children reached the age of thirteen or fourteen.

Single parents can greatly reduce the burden that their children experience by,

- Ensuring that the child is surrounded by a stable network of adults,

- Nurturing their child's sense of helpfulness rather than her conscientiousness,

- Encouraging the child to play with other children as much as possible,

- Directly acknowledging and appreciating the child's feelings of responsibility

And by saying, "I know it worries you that I am a bit depressed at the moment, but I have someone I can talk to about it, so I am sure that things will soon get better. Thanks for your concern!" This is a much better explanation than "Don't you worry about that, dear. Everything will be all right as long as we have each other."

It's also helpful to remember that being alone with children has a negative as well as a positive side, and children experience the closeness and greater contact as both a privilege and an obligation.

To determine whether children experience their over-responsibility as a burden—or, to put it another way, whether their willingness to cooperate is undermining their integrity—watch for the following signs:

- Exaggerated consideration toward the parent and reluctance o spend time with peers

- A tendency to get into conflicts and be contrary

- Forgetfulness concerning carrying out duties and maintaining agreements

- Destructive or aggressive behavior at nursery school or school

- Frequent headaches, stomachaches, back and shoulder pains

- Total rebellion (in adolescence)

- Introversion, melancholy, and social withdrawal

From my experience, these are the most common signs, but this does not necessarily mean that children who do not demonstrate these signs are not over-responsible, nor that all children who do demonstrate them are over-responsible.

Over the past ten years, we have seen an upsurge in over-responsible children, particularly in countries in which national crises and wars divide families and kill off fathers. The seriousness of this phenomenon has led both professionals and parents to profess what I consider to be an exaggerated belief—that children who have become over-responsible can be relieved of this propensity at a later age.

Example: A young mother lived alone with Carl, her eight-year-old son, from his birth until he turned five. At that time she started living with a man whom she had been dating for three years. The mother and her boyfriend were both well educated and interested in children. When they moved in together, they agreed that Carl, who was somewhat over-responsible, should "be allowed to be a child again."

As a result, the two adults embarked on a conscious, goal-directed course of upbringing that was based on the idea that they would make "responsible adult decisions" regarding bedtimes, homework, and extracurricular activities, and that they would "set limits."

After another three years had passed, the mother decided to break off the relationship, partly because the man's view of her son and his ideas about upbringing were more conservative than she thought reasonable.

In the intervening three years, Carl had become overweight and rather quick-tempered, both at home and at school. Now that he was alone with his mother again, violent conflicts occurred almost every day— Carl angrily accused his mother of not loving him anymore.

Naturally both Carl and his mother were dismayed by this state of affairs. Things improved rapidly when Carl was helped to see that when he said to his mother, "You don't love me anymore!" what he really meant was, "I don't feel happy about the way you love me."

The adults in Carl's life had been thoughtful, but misguided. They had overlooked the fact that Carl felt overly responsible not for himself, but toward his mother. Naturally, it did not help Carl when the adults in his life assumed more responsibility for him.

When children like Carl assume too much responsibility at such an early age, this quality becomes an integral part of their personality and cannot simply be amputated. It is possible to check its growth and to prevent it from being misused and exploited, but for children like Carl over-responsibility will continue to be a lifelong tendency that will characterize their relationships with people who are important to them.

Carl's mother and her boyfriend could have done two things that would have helped both Carl and themselves. First, they could have concentrated on making both their individual adult lives and their life together work as well as possible—that is, they could attend to their personal responsibility. The happier Carl's mother was with her adult life, the more he would be able to relax and concentrate his energy on his own childhood. Instead, Carl became the object of their conflicts and the instrument of their breakup, and this outcome ultimately caused his sense of over-responsibility to swell.

Furthermore, they could have encouraged and stimulated the child in him: his irrationality, wildness, unreasonableness, childishness, playfulness, immediacy, and spontaneity.

They intended to give him the "right to be a child," but instead they ended up "playing adults."

In turn, Carl's response to his mother was direct and competent: "If that's the way you want to love me, then I don't want anything to do with it!"

Those children who express themselves more dramatically than Carl—by refusing to clean their rooms, do their homework, babysit younger siblings, help with chores, or go on errands for adults— find themselves in more difficult straits. In addition to shouldering the responsibility for the well-being of the adults, they are criticized and reproached by the adults for being irresponsible when it comes to practical matters.

But children are unable to protest directly when they feel overly responsible. Their only alternative is to dig in their heels on the home front and deal with their pain when they are out of the house. Others are removed by court order, or leave home voluntarily; many others receive support from society in the form of school psychological services, placement in special schools, and counseling.

Teachers, therapists, and foster parents need to understand that they cannot "cure" over-responsibility. I don't mean to be overly pessimistic. But to think otherwise is to add insult to injury.

When children spend the first five, ten, or thirteen years of their lives repressing themselves in order to give priority to their parents' needs and feelings, over-responsibility becomes a central part of their identity and the only way in which they have learned how to be of value to other people. To tell children that they can overcome this way of being hurts their self-esteem and impedes the development of their social responsibility. In fact, when other adults take the place of parents and with the best of intentions start to work on a child's over-responsibility, one of two things will happen:

1. The child will experience this new approach as a criticism of a core quality and either refuse to cooperate or become aggressive, uncooperative, or passive.

2. The child's already well-trained sense of over-responsibility will be reactivated with new adults as its targets. The child's sense of over-responsibility will remain undiminished. The only difference will

be that he or she has become controlled by a new source of external authority with another set of demands and expectations.

The antithesis of over-responsibility is personal responsibility and self-esteem. It is not the task of adults to break down or treat over-responsibility, but to strengthen self-esteem and self-responsibility so that the balance between personal and social responsibility can be restored.

This is a long process. It takes two to three years to initiate, demands patience, and will probably last the rest of the child's life. Both parties need time because the external and internal demands exacted by the process of adaptation are so great in themselves, and because the task facing the child—to find his lost self beneath his strategy for survival—is a difficult one.

Alone with Responsibility

Because many over-responsible children feel as if they are alone with the responsibility for one or both of their parents—or perhaps even for the whole family—they actively seek contact with parents; they are happy when they achieve it, and become frustrated when they don't.

But another group of children from diverse backgrounds is also alone with responsibility. They struggle, often from a very early age, with the task of assuming responsibility for themselves—on their own. It is as if they have concluded, however subconsciously, that their families have nothing to offer them but food, shelter, clothing, and a bed.

As I have mentioned, my experience indicates that these children come from all types of families—from completely ordinary and seemingly healthy families to very problematic families that are lacking in resources. These children have "opted out" because

• Of blatant negligence or physical abuse;

- The parents' problematic relationship has demanded all the family's energy for long periods;

- The family has lacked any real emotional center, and each member has been stranded on his or her own desert island; or

- One of the parents (often the mother) has made exaggerated emotional demands and has only superficially been able to give in return.

As long as they are minors, the main problem facing these children is that they are simply so young. We have no tradition that allows us to perceive of children as self-sufficient beings who do not need to belong to a social group. Therefore we often do not realize the totality of their existential isolation, or we perceive it as merely social loneliness, and this understanding stokes our sentimentality. But on the whole, we just do not see such children at all.

Many of these children grow up without being especially unhappy or even conscious of their circumstances. Often they don't discover their own isolation until they themselves start a family. They seem drawn to people who are used to thriving in relationships. People who grew up by themselves then end up feeling first puzzled and then unhappy about the fact that they have so much difficulty establishing intimate relationships with their partners.

Some children, however, grow up in such destructive families that they develop serious psychological and social problems. They are frustrated because they actually are alone in the world, but they are still hoping and longing for union. Metaphorically speaking, they continue to sit down for dinner with the rest of the family in the hope that food will be served, even though they know that nothing at all will be served, or that they'll only get a helping of empty calories. Their unmet expectations and hopes place them in a painful existential situation where they are isolated and lonely, yet enslaved.

Example:

I encountered a thirteen-year-old boy who had run away from an institution for about the hundredth time. He had been missing for about a month during the middle of winter and had survived by breaking into summer cottages, where he found food and shelter.

I met with him when the police brought him back to the institution.

We talked about his desperate situation, and I attempted, somewhat clumsily, to describe the frustrated relationship he had with his parents, both of whom had problems with alcohol and prescription drugs.

"Well," he said after some time, "I think I know what you mean. It's like in those summer cottages. When I break into one of them to find something to eat, it's really bloody annoying if there isn't any food. Then I kick the fridge or the wastebasket and move on to the next house. But one day I came to a big house with a cellar and everything. I could see that the owners were rich, and I was certain that I was in luck. But you won't believe this: those people had two rooms in the cellar—a food storage room and a wine cellar—but they were shut up behind sort of barred doors made of iron with big padlocks, and I didn't have any tools to break in with.

"You won't believe this, but I sat there the whole bloody night, staring at all that food that I couldn't get my hands on, and do you think I could pull myself together to move on to another house? No, I bloody well couldn't. I just sat there crying, like the idiot I am!. . . . . . Is that what you mean?"

And, yes that was what I meant.

We need to see these children for who they are, because the kind of help and care they respond to is completely different from the kind that other children and young people need. They don't benefit from adult wisdom and experience; they often turn their back on physical contact. They never ask for help. They manage on their own or demand service or material things. And no sooner do you think that you have established personal contact with them than you become "just another adult." They are immune to pedagogical strategy and instruction; for them, society is an abstraction just like any other community. They have always been responsible for themselves, but they have almost no awareness of their own needs. Their sense of social responsibility is as good as nonexistent.

To help these children, two things must happen. First, they have to see themselves as being virtually parentless and alone with the responsibility for their own lives. This does not mean that they have to confront or break with their parents; rather, they need to face up to the fact that qualities such as responsibility, care, trustworthiness, and stable emotional contact—which are necessary requirements for a proper childhood—do not exist in their family. Initially, when children confront these realities they feel relief and then grief, from which it takes time to recover. Only after this process is complete can children experience the freedom that allows them to assume responsibility for their own lives. Confronting such a loss in a child is a difficult step for many adults to take. It is often hard for them to see such stark loneliness in children.

The next step—disregarding most of what we know in terms of conventional educational theory and child rearing—is easier. We need to refrain from playing the part of helpers and instead meet these children on their own terms. This means that we must not think that we know what is best for them; we have to have enough respect and patience to stand by while they are allowed to experiment and work things out for themselves. We need to be constantly aware that our contact with them is not, nor can it be, a substitute for what was lacking in their relationship with their parents. Furthermore, we must be willing for our contact with them to be based also on our own uncertainty and helplessness. We need to act out of a sense of humility, and with the knowledge that we all have equal dignity. In this way these children are like all children: the can do many things themselves but they should not do them alone.

Many of these children—those who have not been subjected to serious abuse by their parents or society—hold a good hand. They are used to loneliness and fear. Furthermore, their original, unspoiled "self" is often intact. They need to make contact with this inner core in order to develop a sense of personal responsibility and an acceptable social responsibility, in that order. Social adjustment has never eased anyone's existential pain; at the most, it provides makeshift protection against pain that will inevitably arise in new contexts.

Parental Power

Recently, when I was working in southern Europe, I heard two mothers discussing how they were bringing up their children. One mother was deeply unhappy because the family's eighteen-year-old son, accused of a series of petty thefts along with some friends, was due to appear in court.

After giving her friend a detailed account of the circumstances, the woman said, "I just don't understand it! All the time he went to school, he was such a lovely boy. He was helpful and hardworking and always among the best students in his class. That's why we always allowed him to do so much. . . . We've never denied that boy anything if we could possibly give it to him. If he wanted to go out in the evening, to a club, he went. We allowed him to do everything, because he was such a good and clever boy."

A little later, when the subject of the conversation had changed to the family's fifteen-year-old daughter, the same woman said, "Yes, I suppose I'm treating her in the wrong way, but I don't dare do otherwise. She's not allowed to do anything now. I'm keeping her at home because I'm afraid that she might get into bad company. . . . She protests, of course, and it's probably not right of me to do it, but I can't help it. What can a mother do?"

This mother is genuinely despairing and perplexed. Her belief in doing "the right thing" has been shaken. Had she raised her son and daughter incorrectly? Tens of thousands of parents of gang members, drug addicts, criminals, and young people who have taken their own lives—or attempted to do so—ask themselves the same question every day. In the midst of their terrible powerlessness, whether they have to make a big or a small decision in relation to their children, these parents wonder, "Are we doing the right thing? Is what we are doing good enough?"

Presumably, no one doubts that parents have power over children and that responsible parents implement this power in everyday situations, and during important conflicts. In the same way, adults also have power outside the family, which should comply with the various laws of society.

The ways in which parents exercise their power—over such issues as dress, marriage, religion, and the use of physical force— vary greatly between cultures. Parents who are forced to flee from one culture to another, or who choose to emigrate, often discover that the customs they took for granted in their homeland are now subject to question. People whose moral concepts will brook no ambiguity often have difficulty moving to countries in which the population is more diverse and moral issues may not be so black and white. This clash can cause personal pain for parents, which in turn has a decisive influence on the life of the whole family.

It is also common knowledge that many parents and other adults commonly misuse their power over children for both ideological and psychological reasons. Fortunately, this type of behavior is on the decline in the most well-informed, democratic societies. To a certain extent, it is also on the wane in schools and other institutions.

But I am less concerned with this type of raw power than its more subtle manifestation. My aim here is to isolate the inevitable balance of power between children and adults and to generate some guidelines according to which adults can assume responsibility for the ways in which they exercise power over children. To me, such guidelines constitute an ethical principle. From a health perspective, these ethical considerations are more relevant than most of the morality that traditionally forms the basis for discussions about how to bring up children.

The guidelines I propose are neither an indictment of certain parents nor evidence of their guilt. It is a discussion of how we all share the responsibility for our children's development and fate. Taking this joint responsibility also naturally means sharing in the blame. The same applies to our adult partners in loving relationships. (As far as I am aware, it applies to our relationships with other people in general, but within the confines of the family, the immediate consequences are particularly apparent and important.)

INTERACTION

In family therapy we explain interaction by saying that the interactive process in a family (or between partners) can have three qualities. Sometimes the interaction between members of a family is constructive and life-giving, at other times it can be destructive, and on occasions we tend to tread water. Or to formulate is in more clinical terms, interaction within families is either:

1. Healing symptoms – i.e. self-destructive behavior learned in the families of origin.

2. Creating symptoms

3. Maintaining or reinforcing symptoms

In most families the interaction naturally contains all three of these qualities, but in different proportions at different times during the course of the family's history. This is the true power of parents no matter how powerless they might feel at times.

It is precisely the quality of what takes place between us that determines how the family prospers. Whether a family malfunctions or flourishes is a function of the in-teraction of family members and not of the actions of one individual.

As most people are aware, interaction consists not only of what can be seen directly in facial expressions and gestures, and what can be heard in words and tone of voice, but also of what can be read "between the lines" in the form of implicit attitudes, feelings, conflicts, and our whole personal background. In family therapy we distinguish between content and process; between *what* we do and say, and *how* we do and say it. Traditionally, we have learned to believe that the content of what we do or say is most important. This is not correct. When content and process are consistent, the two factors assume equal importance. But when this is not the case, process is more important.

The majority of us have grown up in families with parents who were convinced that what they told us—the moral code they gave us and the rules they made for our behavior—determined the quality of our upbringing. If they had high moral standards, they made sure that they adhered to the same rules they laid down for their children.

Perhaps they were aware of an occasional contradiction between attitude and behavior—such as when a father shouts to a son, "Stop shouting!"—and regretted these inconsistencies. Perhaps they worried that they were being ineffective. They also knew that there was a certain correlation between the quality of the parents' relationship to each other and how their children grew up. If the father drank or the mother stole, or the parents were always arguing and fighting, it was likely that the children would fail to thrive and/or would become uncontrollable.

But the parents were not aware that the quality of the process was crucial for the success or failure of their good intentions. They only knew that it was important to do the "right thing," and that when that failed it was because something was wrong with their children, or their children's friends. Or perhaps it was the will of God, testing or teaching them. When they questioned their own efforts, they asked themselves, "Haven't we been strict enough?

Should we have seen things coming and intervened at an earlier stage?" Like the mother with the eighteen-year-old son, they thought about what they had done or failed to do, and not about how they had done it.

In a loving relationship between two equal adults, both have equal responsibility for the quality of the interaction. But adults have complete responsibility for the quality of their interaction with children. This applies to the interaction between children and parents in a family, and between adults and children in nursery schools, day care, schools, and in society.

When I say that adults need to take responsibility for the interaction, I do not mean that they need to take the child's side. What I mean is that even though children and young people influence the process in the interaction with adults, children are not capable of assuming responsibility for it. When children have to take the responsibility for the interaction, they do not develop in healthy ways. This is why children need adult leadership.

Only recently have we begun to understand the factors that need to be present so that children will thrive. The problem is that the way in which we, as adults, influence this process is to a great extent beyond our control. We influence it via our personality (our conscious and subconscious conflicts with ourselves and each other); via the feelings and moods we ignore or repress (the changes of mood we ourselves fail to detect); and via our exaggerated desire to do the right thing and our fear of doing the wrong thing—to mention just a few of the factors.

This is the power we have over our children. Irrespective of what qualities they may have been born with, we have power over the interactive processes that determine their development and quality of life, until they themselves become adults and take over.

In other words, having high moral standards and trying to do what is "right" cannot guarantee that our children will turn out well, as our parents and grandparents believed. **We must abandon the whole idea that it is at all possible to do "what is right."**

Instead, we must develop a code of ethics for our relationships with children according to which we keep our ears and eyes open for the blunders that we inevitably make, and openly assume responsibility for them. This is the only ethical practice that can set children free so that they can develop in healthy ways. Help is available—from our children themselves, in the form of the competent feedback they give us whenever we reach an impasse.

Let me return to that unhappy mother and her dilemma concerning her son who was awaiting trial on some petty thefts. She and her husband had brought him up according to the old formula: if the boy is shaping up well, he should be praised and rewarded—if not, crack down on him and restrict his freedom.

In the culture in which this family lives, the parents have no doubt about the content of their interaction with their children: it is a question of bringing up their children to be nice and hardworking and clever at school, and otherwise doing what their parents tell them to do. The ideal is for children to adapt and to subject themselves to external control. If content and process had been in harmony—if the son's "good behavior" had been a reflection of his good feeling about himself—he would have become a nice young man who worshipped his mother, and who enjoyed a beer or two with his father at Sunday lunch.

But things did not turn out that way. There was a missing element in the interaction: his parents had emphasized their son's achievements and forgotten about his "being." (Actually they had not forgotten about it; they had merely overlooked its importance. Because they were successful themselves, they assumed that social success automatically produces existential contentment.) In such cases, applying the externally controlled ideal in child rearing suddenly becomes dangerous. Thus the boy stands there with his good grades, his low self-esteem, his lack of self-responsibility, and his longing for any kind of social identity whatsoever, as long as it does not resemble that of his parents. In time, he turns to bad company—his thieving friends—and they assume power over him in the same way his parents wanted to: if you do as we do, you're one of us; if you do not, you're out in the cold!

The mother was correct in assuming that her daughter will not fare much better even though she uses the reverse strategy with the girl. In their culture, the daughter would most likely either start to do badly in school, fight with her parents, or get pregnant so that she can leave home.

Children cooperate in relation to both the constructive and the destructive processes in their family: their psyche does not allow them to differentiate one from the other. Gradually, as their consciousness, language, and values develop, they become able to reject their parents' destructive behavior. Even so, it gets under their skin and becomes a part of their personality.

Therefore, when children start to behave destructively or self-destructively (depending on whether they cooperate straightforwardly or invertedly), it is possible to assume three things about their situation with a great degree of certainty:

1. Their destructive/self-destructive behavior does not originate with them. It always starts with the adults in their life.

2. The adults in the family are generally not conscious of their destructive/self-destructive behavior and are in that sense blameless.

3. The destructive/self-destructive behavior of the child has developed over a number of years, even though the parents may be able to identify a recent incident in the child's life that appears to have sparked the behavior. (Infants often react more immediately.)

It is not possible for us to abdicate our adult power, and there are limits as to how much we can prepare ourselves to exert this power for two reasons: we know too little about ourselves, and all children are different. Often it is impossible to know who our child was, and who we were, until long after the child has left home.

THE RESPONSIBLE USE OF POWER

How can parents use their power responsibly in terms of their children's physical, economic, and social well-being? I think we can all agree that parents are entitled to use physical power to prevent a three-year-old from running into the middle of the street, or to take a sick child to the doctor. Likewise, parents are forced to consider their family's economic situation as a whole and with regard to the future; therefore, at certain times, they have to use their economic power. Similarly, parents need to decide whether a baby should be placed in day care, and which school a child should attend—exerting, in this way, their social power.

Conflicts first arise when our parental responsibility begins to compete with, or completely overtakes, children's personal responsibility. Traditionally, this happens with regard to the issues of food, sleep, school, clothing, homework, pocket money, and getting up in the morning. There is also a "gray zone" regarding issues of cleaning up, personal hygiene, and how much time children need to spend with family members such as uncles, aunts, and grandparents. In this gray zone, children's personal responsibility must be invited, talked over, and negotiated when it conflicts with the way the parents see their parental responsibility.

How should parents handle conflicts that involve a clash between parental responsibility and children's personal responsibility? I will explore a few examples in order to suggest approaches and consequences. My goal is to establish some guidelines that can be used when doubts arise as to what is actually happening in a family, and how beneficial or healthy it is for all parties concerned.

Let's start with a common conflict: should parents wake children in the morning or let them wake themselves up? The answer is that children older than five can wake themselves. Yet in most families, the older the child, the more wake-up calls she needs. Why?

There are two reasons. First, many parents are taking a contradictory position: they wake their children, but at the same time they tell them that they ought to be able to get up on their own. Second, the children are cooperating with their parents—by becoming helpless and dependent.

In this example, personal responsibility meets parental responsibility. Obviously, children should assume personal responsibility for waking themselves up and getting themselves to school. On the other hand, the parents are held accountable if children arrive at school late. What can parents do? The answer is simple. Do what suits you best. If you can wake your children with peace of mind and a smile on your face, and they actually get up, then by all means, carry on.

If, on the other hand, you are unable to do so, then it is sensible to stop. If you have to call your children three, four, or seven times before they get out of bed, and you become irritated and stressed, and the day begins with bad feelings, then you are receiving the signal I mentioned earlier. Your family indicator is telling you that you are in the midst of a "destructive conflict": a conflict that repeats itself with increasing regularity during which the exchanges between the parties involved become increasingly negative, taking the form of criticism, reproach, accusations, abusive language, irony, and sarcasm.

When the interaction takes a negative direction, it always means that the parents have exceeded their own limits. They have forsaken their personal responsibility and assumed responsibility that belongs to their children. The real problem isn't whether the children can wake themselves up and get to school. If held responsible, the children will probably oversleep a couple of times at first and perhaps even try to pretend to put the responsibility back on their parents, but that will soon pass. No, the real problem is that when parents choose to assume a responsibility that really belongs to the children, they become accountable for the destructive conflict that ensues. They have the obligation to hand back the responsibility to their children.

But it is at this precise juncture that many parents tend to act in a very irresponsible way: they blame the children for the conflict.

How should the situation be handled? If parents choose to take the responsibility in this situation and at the same time give children a model of how to assume personal responsibility, they need to sit down with their children and say something like this:

"Now listen. When you were young, we thought it was nice to wake you up in the mornings, so we took the responsibility of making sure that you got up. But we don't think so anymore. In fact, we feel irritated almost every day. So now we've decided to give the responsibility for this back to you. If now and again you go to bed late and are worried that you won't hear the alarm clock, then you just have to tell us and we'll help you. But otherwise you'll have to make sure you get up every morning from now on."

In this way the responsibility has been returned to the children to whom it belongs, in a caring but definitive way. No one has been blamed, and the parents have set a good example for their children. Most important, the destructive process has been removed and replaced by a constructive one—the effects of which have many more significant implications for a child's future than whether she is late for school a couple of times.

The same template can be followed if parents want children to put themselves to bed at a reasonable hour—another area of frequent disagreement. Children are perfectly capable of controlling their own bedtimes. If given the opportunity, they will do what their parents do: get enough sleep most of the time, but sometimes, just like their parents, get too little because they are occupied with an important task, are enjoying themselves, or are watching something on television.

But I do not mean that children should decide about their bedtimes if parents prefer to have it otherwise. Irrespective of whether parents choose a bedtime because they want peace and quiet for themselves, or because they want to make sure that their children get enough rest, or for some other completely different reason, parents can use their power and exert their parental responsibility.

Again, in this case, they alone bear the responsibility if the interaction develops destructively. It is also their responsibility to change their decision or their attitude when destructive conflicts begin to materialize in connection with bedtimes. Parents have to assume responsibility, because the conflict is much more detrimental to the children's health than a few missed hours of sleep. Remember, process overrides content; the quality of interaction overrules attitude and method.

It's essential that parents distinguish between "destructive conflicts" and ordinary conflicts, which are simply a question of parents and children wanting different things. The latter type of conflict is not unhealthy. The fact that children often say, "Oh, can't I stay up a little longer to-night?" is a sign of both their own and the family's health. Parents have historically been willing to entertain such requests—they haven't created an atmosphere where such questions are forbidden.

Parents can answer yes or no at their discretion, or they can enter into some kind of agreement depending on the situation.

If the child begins in a more defensive manner, "Oh, why do I always have to go to bed so early?" then the answer should be, "Because that's the way I want it to be!" (Remember that the parent takes the responsibility.) Or the parent and child may reach an agreement. But parents should not say, "Because you are tired and have to get up in the morning." It is one thing to take over a child's personal responsibility, but quite another to monopolize and define his needs and feelings.

The fact that children are very often aware of what they would like to do but not what they need does not mean that parents always know what their children need. So if the child says, "Yes, but I'm not at all sleepy!"—the answer is, "Well, I can understand that you think it's annoying, but I still want you to go to bed." This can be said even if the child's eyes are nothing but small tiny pinholes and her shoulders are drooping down to her knees.

just as it is decisive for the quality of interaction that adults assume responsibility for themselves, it is also important that they not back out of conflicts. Conflicts are not in themselves dangerous for the health of a family. It is the way in which conflicts unfold that can be dangerous.

Let's consider another area in which conflicts frequently arise— homework—and try to examine this issue in some detail to identify the factors influencing the interactive process.

After three or four years of school, many parents find that their initial interest in their child's schoolwork begins to wane. That's when they revert to the automatic parental answering machine that says things such as

- "Did you have a nice day at school today?"

- "Have you got any homework for tomorrow? You haven't? It seems to me that you never have any homework. Are you sure?"

Interest is replaced by control, which can be detected in a parent's tone of voice, facial expressions, and body language. The process has changed from warmth to coolness, from making contact to creating distance. Control creates irresponsibility and distance promotes indifference.

What happens next depends on the circumstances. If the child loves going to school and looks upon homework as a treasured duty, very little will change. If not, there is a good chance that daily conflicts will arise at homework time. Kids may tell white lies, cheat, and bring home letters from the teacher.

With regard to homework, parents are in a dilemma. Teachers seem to have decided that completing homework is the responsibility of the parents. This is both illogical and inappropriate, and it puts children and parents in an impossible situation. Some children and parents learn how to tackle this situation and cooperate well together. But many others flounder.

Logically, homework is a matter between pupil and teacher. Parents should be free to take an interest in a child's homework and help when necessary. This type of interaction would give children a wonderful opportunity to develop their self-responsibility (for their own learning) as well as their social responsibility (in relation to teachers), and it would allow parents the opportunity to exercise their parental responsibility by intervening between child and teacher when conflicts arise. Unfortunately, parents are instead reduced to acting like an extension of the teacher.

Until this situation changes, parents and children will continue to develop destructive conflicts in connection with homework. If this happens, the same strategy should be used as I have described with regard to children getting up on time: give the responsibility back to the children to whom it belongs.

If parents have assumed responsibility for homework for some time, the period of transition can be difficult for both parties. It is hard for the child to reassume his self-responsibility, and no less problematic for parents to relinquish their control. But all of a sudden it happens!

One glorious day, the parents will feel free to express their genuine interest in their child's schoolwork in a way that does not cause their child to turn off. And on another glorious day, the miracle actually takes place: you ask your twelve-year-old son if he has a lot of homework to do for the following day, and he answers, "Yes, piles! But I've decided to go down to the harbor and do some fishing instead. It's just the day for fishing!"

When that day comes, the problem has been solved. He has re-gained his self-responsibility, and he is in a position to give priority to his well-being on occation rather than his duties, and he can express this without resorting to cheating or lying. Many parents will find this a difficult mouthful to swallow—the automatic parental answering machine will be tempted to spit forth messages full of dire warnings, and of the difficulties of getting a job after leaving school. But my recommendation is to celebrate—big time! Just think of how many days in a child's life are spend with what others expect and demand of him. A few fishing trips during all those years does not turn anybody into a derelict or a looser.

The school might disagree with this and blame you for your supporting your child and that is the time to remind yourself that school possesses loads og knowledge but not neccesarily wisdom.

Parents need to assume active responsibility by allowing their children to take responsibility instead of giving up in passive resignation when faced with these perpetual conflicts. This active responsibility puts a stop to destructive conflicts, whereas resignation ("It's no good saying anything!") simply reduces the volume of the conflict.

Parents exert different facets of their power on many occasions every day in relation to matters both great and small. That is the way it has to be. Until adolescence, children need parents who have the courage to take the lead and who can act on the basis of their greater knowledge, insight, and experience as sparring partners, decision makers, and the executors of power.

All of these decisions, great and small, make an impression on children, and if the children are healthy they will respond verbally, emotionally, and physically. They will become happy, unhappy, furious, hurt, and pleased; they will disagree, and be critical; in short, they will call upon the full spectrum of their mental and emotional reactions. When we are most fortunate and our relationship with our children functions at its best, we receive spontaneous, personal feedback so that we always know where we stand with them.

In the old familiar patriarchal family, the so-called positive reactions were permitted, but the so-called negative ones were prohibited. "Negative" feelings were described as such because the environment did not approve of them, not because they were bad for those who had them. Today we realize that these feelings are only "bad" when they are not expressed.

The tradition is, therefore, that children's negative reactions to their parents' exertion of power have been either repressed, condemned, or criticized. There are then two consequences: either the repression is successful and the child loses her self-esteem and becomes submissive; or, as the child grows older, these restrained reactions begin to express themselves in an explosive way, creating more negative responses.

The spontaneous reactions of children and young people are the nearest we can get to a true expression of their integrity and character—of their very being. The classical, critical way that adults have reacted to children's self-expression is therefore a violation of the children's integrity.

We can use our economic, physical, and social power either to give or to deny children what they are in need of, but when we use our power to rule that their reactions and feelings are "wrong," we are abusing our power. Our status as parents does not give us the right to violate life itself. Exactly the same ethical rules apply to our relationships with other adults.

In summary, consider these reactions by a parent to a child who is sputtering with anger and frustration because she couldn't get what she wanted:

- "Now stop that showing off or I'll make sure that you really get something to howl about!" (In its most primitive form, this comment is accompanied by a couple of slaps and marching orders.)

- "Now listen. I don't like you getting upset like this. I'm sorry, but I mean no. I just can't accept it." (In its most advanced form, the reaction would be: "Oh, dear! I didn't realize it meant so much to you. Come here and explain to me why it's so important.")

Neither adults nor children can thrive when uninitiated adults condemn spontaneous manifestations of their being. In this connection, the only difference between children and adults is that for a few years in their lives, children are under the impression that the world was created for them and that their parents are omnipotent and perfect. They will soon enough learn that this is not the way things are; they don't need to be humiliated in the process.

LIMITS

Throughout history, parents have had problems getting children to respect family limits governing behavior and personal expression, and today's parents are no exception. In fact, we may have a harder time setting limits with our children than our parents and grandparents did. In the "good old days," limits were synonymous with the internal rules of the family, which were defined by the adults and which children had to follow. Often these rules coincided with the limits set by the larger society, making them easier to enforce. But as society becomes much more diverse, the gap between family and societal limits has widened, making setting limits harder.

Yet from another perspective, setting limits is as hard today as it was years ago because limits tend to be enforced in ways that violate children's integrity. **As a result, children do not learn to respect the integrity of other people. Instead, they learn to fear their power.**

Over the past thirty years, children and young people have undergone a collective consciousness-raising. They are less fearful and respectful of authority, and as a result the goal of achieving relationships between adults and children that are based on equal dignity has moved one step closer. In this sense, the old notion of setting limits has outlived its usefulness. Adults can still impose limits, of course, but to do so means that they must abuse their power, or manipulate and take advantage of children's basic desire to cooperate with the adults they trust and upon whom they depend.

I am not disputing the old notion that children need limits/rules in order to feel secure. Just like every family needs a handful of rules in order to function as smoothly as possible. Rather I urge readers to think of limits as something other than a "one size fits all" set of rules.

Previously, adults placed limits on children – like a fence around them.

Fig. 4

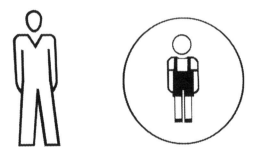

In contrast, I propose that adults define their personal boundaries – being clear about who they are.

Fig. 5

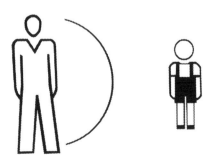

There is no universally applicable set of rules. Adults must learn to establish their own individual, personal limits and boundaries in their interactions with children.

Adults, in other words, need to assume their own personal authority, not authoritarian power. The task will be easiest for those who grew up in families that respected their integrity. Those who were not so fortunate—who suffered through years of repressing their own thoughts and feelings—will have to practice developing their own sense of personal responsibility and speaking in their own personal language either in their relationship with their children or in the context of loving relationships with other adults.

DISCARDING ROLES

Until quite recently, it was taken for granted that adults assumed various roles in relation to children: they functioned as father, mother, teacher, grandmother, and so forth. Each of these roles had its own attitude, body language, and vocabulary, which, of course, were colored by each person's individual personality and current social stereotypes.

Children in today's free societies have limited respect for these stereotypical adult roles. I would venture to say that young people have become our equals more quickly than we have become theirs. To my way of thinking, this development will prove advantageous to parents and children both individually and in terms of their relationship with each other.

But while we are in the midst of this transition, children's lack of what we used to understand as respect has created some severe conflicts similar to those that characterized relations between men and women when women began to insist on their right to be treated with equal respect. Power struggles between parents and children are raging in some families; in others, parents have become so resigned that their sporadic attempts to inspire respect seem empty and ineffective. Still more families are coping with children who develop symptomatic or problematic behavior.

What can these families do? From my perspective, all children—regardless of whether they are acting out in their quest for limits—need to be treated with respect. Parents are not free to violate their children's integrity, self-esteem, or self-responsibility. Instead parents need to act in a way that seems paradoxical. If children want limits, it seems natural that parents should give them limits—that is, that parents should embrace their traditional, authoritarian roles as "mother" and "father." But I advise the opposite. I suggest that parents discard these roles and instead begin to build up their own personal authority.

This is not easy. It takes time for parents to eliminate defensive regret, reproach, and criticism from their expressions and tone of voice, especially if they feel as if their children have been trying their patience. Because of the inherent difficulty of this undertaking, some parents settle on a solution that appears easier and corresponds to the classical parental role: they supplement their role as the family's absolute authority with some modern negotiating techniques and educational theories. This is also a dangerous solution. It confuses adult self-respect with vanity, and equates the needs children have for warmth and contact with their need for rules and structure.

Some parents are loathe to shed their traditional roles because doing so feels as if they're giving up something valuable, especially if the role has become a refuge for them in that it confirms their value as responsible adults. These parents have simply learned that the only true and loving way in which they can be parents is to be authoritarian. Shedding this role inaugurates a period of great personal uncertainty; they feel naked, stripped bare, and as if they are not living up to their parental responsibilities. Yet often their children feel more comfortable; in fact, they thrive—because their parents seem more genuine and present.

To begin this role-shedding process, listen to what the automatic parental answering machine says in different situations that arise with children. And then ask yourself:

- Is that what I really think, or do I think something else?

- How much of what I say do I actually agree with based on my own attitudes and experience?

- Which of my comments are superfluous? Which have I inherited from my parents and grandparents?

- How often do I say things to my children that hurt me when my parents said them to me?

- How much do I say and do things out of loyalty toward my partner?

- What things do I say because I heard teachers or other adults say them?

- Now take a few days to carefully observe your children, and listen to them as they talk about their daily lives. Then ask yourself:

- When do I see a glint of pain in their eyes?

- When do they lift their chins as a sign of self-defense?

- When do they tense their backs in anger and defiance?

- When does their energy intensify and become aggressive?

- When do their eyes become clear and their bodies relax?

- When are they happy and secure?

- When do they look as though they have just scored a success?

- When they cry, is it out of natural frustration or are they emotionally distressed?

Most parents who ask themselves these questions realize that they are carrying around two versions of their children: the children who actually exist, and the children who exist in their minds. Compare the two. Determine whether your preconceived ideas about raising children coincide with the information you have gathered from your children. Talk to your children, your partner, and your friends. And then ask yourself:

- How do I appear to others?

- How do they perceive me?

- Who do I perceive myself to be?

- From what source do I derive my opinions and attitudes?

- Which opinions and attitudes represent my true values, and which should I consider dropping?

- How nervous am I about the reactions of others if I change my opinions and attitudes?

- Do I dare to stand alone as I am, or would I rather adapt myself?

- What have I said recently that others thought was strange, hurtful, or superfluous? Do I share their opinion?

We cannot discard our roles in a single day, nor is it necessary for us to do so. We can begin slowly. Children sense when their parents start to take themselves seriously, and they respond by changing their behavior almost as quickly. Even if parents change how they act only because they want their children to behave "properly," children notice the shift and change their behavior. But if parents aren't sincere—if they initiate these changes only for "their children's sake"—then children revert back to their old behavior.

Setting Limits

Most of us wish to establish two types of limits with our children.

The limits in the first group remain relatively stable, whereas those in the other group change according to our state of mind.

The list of stable limits could go on and on because it contains items that parents—in almost every culture—generally think of as enriching or protecting their children's lives:

- I want you to take your shoes off before you come into the living room.

- I want you to clear up your toys before you go to bed.

- I want you to go to church with me until you are old enough to make up your own mind about religion.

- I want to have a say in what you watch on television.

It is a great advantage to use a personal language ("I want . . .") when setting these limits instead of resorting to absolute terms, such as "You're not allowed to go into the living room with your shoes on," or "It's not good for you to see everything on TV at your age." There are several reasons for this. When rules are expressed personally rather than as general "truths" or rules, they have more meaning for children, and children respect both the limit and the person expressing the limit much more. Children, as well as adults, tend to feel small, irresponsible, wrong, stupid, and in need of correction when they are constantly barraged by rules. And when children feel respected, they are much more willing to cooperate.

The second type of limit is personal and idiosyncratic.

- I don't want you to play the piano now. I want some peace.

- I would like to read you a story later, but right now I want to talk to your mother.

- Today I want the bathtub to myself.

- I don't want you on my lap now. You'll have to move.

- I don't want you to take my books off the shelf.

- I'm having one of those days when I wish that I didn't have a family at all! I want to be left alone, unless the house catches fire!

- I don't want you to play with my makeup today.

It's the personal language itself that carries the message. The particular emotion given voice to is of less importance. Words can hurt us; genuine emotions do not. There is nothing wrong with a parent expressing sadness, anger, giddiness, humor, or irritation. It does not matter that children sometimes "feel rejected" if a parent says something that is rejecting. In this way they learn that they cannot always get what they want, and that individuals exist within the context of family life. In other words, other people in the family have their own individual needs too.

There's another reason why we shouldn't shy away from expressing our true feelings in personal language: our individual temperaments, feelings, and emotional ups and downs are a part of who we are. Therefore, information about these qualities is not merely a legitimate part of the message; it is a desirable part as well. Language defines limits; expressing feelings maintains a warmth of contact. We often forget that the warmth that exists in any relationship arises from two sources: what joins us together and what causes friction. Both are always present, and both can be equally warm.

Personal language—"I want," "I don't want," and so forth—only works if it really is personal. If it is undermined, used for other purposes, or used as a linguistic trick, such as merely replacing "You" with "I," it ceases to be effective. Those parents who grew up in families in which personal language was forbidden or considered unsuitable need time to rediscover this form of expression, but it is worth the effort. It is invaluable in rescuing not only our relationships with our children, but our relationships with spouses, parents, colleagues, superiors—and ourselves.

When parents and other adults set personal limits, they are primarily protecting their own needs. When they can do so without violating the needs of children, the interactive process in the family benefits as well. Setting personal limits appropriately is characterized not only by a fundamental respect for the variety of life, but also by respectful practice. Children learn about the value of human respect and consideration not simply in the form of a moral commandment; they also learn how to act ethically and with emphaty. During this learning process they will often be frustrated and that is ok. Frustration is an integral part of learing.

Yet, as we all know, none of us is perfect. We cannot always live up to our good intentions. We cannot always avoid violating each other's limits, and we inevitably hurt and humiliate one another. This is an inevitable part of being human and belonging to a family. But even such violations are not harmful to children unless they communicate self-righteousness and blame.

When Setting Limits Goes Awry

As I have already mentioned, one of the fundamental family problems has always been that parents and other adults enforce limits in ways that violate children's integrity. This poses a problem to both adults and children: adults do not always get the respect they want, and children get caught in the contradiction they perceive between the values their parents profess and the way their parents actually behave.

For example, two-year-old Peter and his parents are visiting good friends. As is customary in their circle, Peter's parents have not brought any toys with them for the child to play with. He is expected to sit quietly. Ninety minutes into the visit, he is permitted to walk around a little on his own.

He sees a hammer lying on the kitchen table and picks it up enthusiastically. His parents react immediately: "Peter! You mustn't do that!" his mother says. His father adds, "Peter! Listen to what your mother says. Put it down! You can't play with adult tools."

Incidents like this happen in every family. The only aspect that varies is the degree to which the child's integrity is violated:

- "You mustn't play with that hammer, Peter! How many times do I have to tell you?" (that is, How stupid can you be?!)

- "You mustn't play with that hammer, Peter! When will you learn to listen to what's said to you?" (that is, Your appetite for the world is a sign of disloyalty toward your parents!)

- "You mustn't play with that hammer, Peter! You're old enough to understand that, aren't you, dear?" (that is, You're a little twerp!)

In all probability, Peter has heard what they said, but he is completely absorbed. He proceeds to swing the hammer in the air as he walks toward his father. When he drops the hammer on the floor, his father gives him a slap in the face. Peter holds his breath and then bursts into tears. His father reacts by slapping the boy's hand and dragging him up onto his lap, while demanding that Peter stop crying. Peter starts to sob quietly. His parents nod to each other in confirmation. Five minutes later, Peter eases off his father's lap and looks at the others with bright eyes and a cautious, searching smile.

The limits had been set ("You mustn't play with the hammer"), the law was broken, and the sentence has been carried out. What has Peter learned? He will never gain respect for his parents' limits, but he will learn to fear the punishment. Furthermore, he will learn that it is wrong to express his pain. And he will grow up feeling that his father demands respect from him but does not feel the need to treat him with respect. This treatment creates an untenable inequality between the child and the adult. In effect, what Peter's father has said to his son is, "You must respect my limits, but I do not need to respect yours."

In this case, the destructive message ("Respect me even though I don't respect you") assumes more weight than any message Peter might have received about playing with adult tools. Each time his father criticizes him, Peter feels increasingly wrong—and the more children feel that they are in the wrong, the more difficult it is for them to do something right. **Whenever a particular learning process is accompanied by a negative emotional experience learning slows down or stops. The only alternative is for the child to become emotionally numb.**

Peter's father could have prevented this dynamic from becoming entrenched by taking the hammer away from Peter and saying, "I don't want you to play with that, Peter." It is possible that Peter would have cried all the same, but his integrity would have remained intact. He would have learned that his father takes both his limits and his forbiddance seriously, and that he is prepared to take an active responsibility to ensure that he is obeyed—principles that children easily respect.

Six-and seven-year-old children who constantly violate adult limits do so because the limits their parents set during the first few years of their life violated their sense of integrity. Parents who continually find themselves saying, "If you only knew how often we've told him about it!" or "We've said it a hundred and one times, but it doesn't help!" are happily oblivious of the fact that the problem is of their own creation.

Parents less authoritarian than Peter's have their own problems setting limits. That's because the democratization of relationships between parents and children has introduced a new and destructive phenomenon into the complexity surrounding setting limits. Some parents were so cautious about issuing old-fashioned orders and restrictions that they ended up ceding responsibility to their children. The following statements send the child the message that he is responsible for setting limits:

- "Mommy would like to hear what Auntie is saying on the phone, Simon!"

- "Simon, Mommy gets upset when you do that with your food. Wouldn't you like to eat properly?"

Whether the tone of these statements is friendly, angry, or pleading, the speaker's intention is the same: to avoid sounding authoritarian. The result, however, is that the child is given the responsibility for establishing the parent's personal limits and well-being. No child can live up to these demands. As a result, children often become more or less hyperactive and chaotic. Ultimately, this leads to the children's immediate desires and needs completely controlling family life—not because they have a thirst for power or feel happy about the state of affairs, but simply because the parents aren't setting limits and taking care of their own needs.

From a linguistic angle, the problem with the statements from the democratic parent is that they are purely passive. They lack an "active" dimension. Each can be rephrased in the active voice. For example:

- "Simon, I want you to be quiet while I'm talking to Auntie."

- "I want you to keep your food on your plate, Simon."

When we use passive phrases, we describe ourselves and our feelings. By using active statements, we assume responsibility for ourselves and our well-being. When we omit the active, self-responsible voice, we give responsibility for ourselves to others. This is unfortunate because no one— neither children nor adults—can ever assume responsibility for us. If we cede responsibility for ourselves to others, we end up feeling as if we are "victims," at the mercy of others.

Try going into a butcher's shop and saying, "I'm hungry!" The butcher will either ignore you or say, "Well, what would you like to eat?"

In family interaction, we also have to assume an active responsibility for ourselves in order to get what we need. A delicate series of balances exists in every family. Passivity fosters polarization. If one parent is passive, for example, the other often compensates by becoming more active.

Some parents find it relatively easy to change their style—precisely because it was only a style. Others find it extremely hard to change the way they communicate because they have suffered through years of repressing their own thoughts and feelings. This makes conversation difficult not only with their children, but with other adults as well.

One parent may be viewed as "too soft," while the other is classified as "hard and inflexible." This is a false way of presenting the problem because this view is based on the belief that there is one "right" way of raising children. There is none. What does exist is a mutual learning process based on who you are as a parent and who your child is. Parents need to learn to be as true to themselves as possible, and as direct and personal in their expression as they can be. By doing so, they will learn about the true nature and personality of each child, and thanks to the child's competent feedback, parents will be able to fine-tune their reactions to the child.

Similarly, there is no set of limits that is universally good for all children. The real question is, "What is good for my relationship with my child?" That is, what makes both of us—and the relationship between us—develop in a healthy way? Remember, there are always three entities to consider: the child, the adult, and their relationship. If one suffers, all three do.

Children can get along quite happily if their parents have different limits. That is, they have no problem learning that their mother doesn't mind if the television is on during dinner cleanup but their father does. Problems only arise if personal limits are transformed into impersonal rules and regulations. When this happens, children become confused because they try to relate to rules. It is much easier to relate to people.

Social Limits

When we consider limits on behavior when children are away from the family, we've entered the realm of social limits. These limits govern children's choices for personal fulfillment outside the home—how they spend their free time, how they play, who they play with, how they get along with friends, boyfriends and girlfriends, and so forth.

Traditionally, children ask for permission to do certain things outside the home, and parents act as authority figures who grant permission or refuse it. I don't question the rights of parents to make the decisions they judge to be best. It is good and necessary that parents exercise this type of power. But this power must be exercised within the context of respecting children's self-esteem and personal responsibility. This means that families need to negotiate and discuss issues before decisions are made.

I often meet parents who take their power almost too literally. In these families, the parents' word passes for law—without discussion. For example, a child asks for permission—"Dad, can I stay at Tracy's place tonight?"—and it is instantly granted or refused: "No, you can't. You've got to stay home."

It would be more constructive for both parties if, by the time children are five or six, the parents refrained from making an immediate decision and asked, "What do you think?" In this way, children learn to examine themselves a bit deeper, to look beyond the immediate desire and enthusiasm that prompted them to ask for permission. They learn to consult themselves instead of focusing all their attention on their parents. Accordingly, their self-esteem and self-responsibility grow, and the ensuing dialogue between parents and child becomes one in which both partners retain equal dignity.

The same applies to decisions about children's social activities. Parents have to decide whether they want to focus on maintaining their power and control, or on developing their children's sense of personal responsibility in the social arena. To accomplish the latter, they need to establish—as carefully and personally as possible, individually and together—what they are prepared to accept and what they are not, just as they do when establishing their own personal limits.

But there are two important differences between personal and social limits. When children are in the outside world, parents have very little influence over what can happen, and as a result they tend to feel much more anxious. Second, in setting social limits, we do so in an area of children's lives in which we ourselves are bystanders, not participants, as we are in family life. We can hope that they will join the Scouts, play football, or take music lessons, and we can encourage them in these directions, but ultimately the decision is theirs. Similarly, we have no influence over one of the most important factors in their lives: friendships.

Adults often underestimate the importance of children's friendships just as we underrate the significance of the love lives of young people. We assure children that they will quickly make new friends if they have to move to another school, and that the world is full of interesting and attractive people to date when their romances turn sour. But we tend to forget the significance of a best friend or a first boyfriend—that these are the first people outside the family to whom our children seriously attach themselves. Friendships and love relationships provide our children with the pivotal experience of learning to trust and relate to others. We do our children a profound disservice when we console them superficially.

Friendships often have a decisive influence on our children's choice of sparetime activities. Sometimes parents deplore this influence. They worry that their child can't make up his own mind about whether to play basketball after school until he consults with his friend. But the fact that children become attached to their friends does not necessarily signal a lack of independence. Rather it is an expression of the fact that friendships and social contacts are more important than the activity itself or the level of achievement. Parents, on the other hand, often focus on the achievement or the activity.

Striking a balance between what we want for our children and what their friends want is often difficult. I am not advocating that parents give way to arguments such as "Everybody else does it," or "All the others are allowed to." Yet parents have resorted to these arguments more and more, especially as the basis for "traditional family values" has begun to erode; that is, they are more likely to compare their own attitudes with those of other parents of children in the same school or local community.

But putting stock in the values of others is a hazardous approach. It's much more beneficial to determine policy by beginning a dialogue with children rather than relying on what other parents think or do. This is easier to do if there is a tradition of negotiation and dialogue within the family. If no such tradition exists, parents who try to institute this approach will be confronted with pressure tactics from their children. Such tactics ultimately erode everyone's self-respect. When children act this way, it's a clear sign to parents that they have been too hasty to legislate.

The solution is not to give in when children mount an overwhelming offensive, but to start teaching the family to negotiate. Often children negotiate in a healthier way than their parents do, even if they express themselves less eloquently or rationally. Seen schematically, there are two models of negotiation:

1. need/desire—>satisfaction—>composure/balance.

In this straightforward paradigm, the child expresses her desire— whether for food, a drink, a trip to the movies, a bedtime story, or a new bicycle—sees that it is fulfilled, and becomes composed.

2. need/desire—>struggle/discussion/dialogue—>defeat/ grief—
    >composure/balance.

In this paradigm, the child expresses her desire and encounters resistance from her parents, which causes her to struggle to have her wish fulfilled. When she is not successful, the child "grieves" (cries, stamps her feet, slams the door, or becomes sulky and introspective). After two minutes, two hours, or perhaps even two days, the child comes to terms with her defeat and regains her balance.

This paradigm—struggling for what we want and grieving when we don't achieve it—is universal; only the outward expression varies from one culture to another. Unfortunately, many parents interpret the struggle and subsequent grief as impolite, disloyal, or immature—but it is not. What parents need to understand is that a child's protests are not directed outwardly at the other party but inwardly, at her own self—they are expressions of personal feelings. We can appeal to each other's common sense and understanding, but such appeals cannot replace the organic process I have outlined; they can only supplement it. Therefore it is important that we do not interrupt children (or other adults) when they are struggling and grieving. It is important that we do not take their reaction personally and make them feel wrong, and it is equally important that we do not become sentimental or lazy and just give in because we cannot stand the struggle or bear the crying.

This process works whether the limits being imposed are personal or social. It is also pertinent to those situations in which we are forced to say no, because we don't have the energy, time, or money to say yes, even though we wish we did.

Children's frustration and grief are not expressions of the fact that we are bad parents. Neither are these expressions of feeling a signal of egoism or lack of loyalty. Instead they are a declaration of children's will and their desire to live harmoniously with us. It is also a demonstration of their confidence in us—that they believe that we want to be with them even when they are emotionally upset. In order to live up to this confidence, we need only meet them with sympathetic silence. As a reward, we will avoid constant minor conflicts and unbearable pestering. The same result can be achieved by exerting our authoritarian power, but this approach carries a high price.

SOCIAL LIMITS AND OLDER CHILDREN

Until age eleven or twelve, children need and want to be with their parents. Eventually, however, their need for contact with their parent's decreases, and their social needs—for contact with their peers and other adults—increase and become increasingly important. This does not mean that family becomes less important for the quality of their lives only that they spend more time with friends.

These emerging social needs raise new questions concerning limits and challenge a number of the well-established norms in the family. Can your child eat dinner at a friend's house or must he come home for dinner? Can he play with a friend all day Saturday, or should he spend some of the weekend with the family? Questions such as these put children's self-responsibility to the test for the first time outside the family. It's also the first opportunity parents have to receive feedback about how successfully they have brought up their children.

When I reached this age, I had to establish a double life, just as many children brought up in traditional families did. Because our parents insisted on exercising control over our lives, we created one life that they knew about, and one that remained a secret from them. This made everyday life somewhat exciting, but the price was steep: we learned to lie, to suppress the truth, and to be irresponsible. We also felt ashamed of who we were. Naturally, this corrupted our relationship with our parents. But even worse, we incorporated these aspects of daily life into our personality, and they had a destructive influence on us, interfering with our attempts to live up to the demands of being responsible partners and parents.

Today's children have more freedom in their relationship with their parents, and they are less prepared to tolerate lies and abuses of power. These twin factors place greater demands on the quality of the decision-making processes undertaken by children and parents.

Previously, parents alone decided on a curfew, for example. If the child was dissatisfied with it, he either put up with it or came home late and accepted the punishment. Today it is much more difficult for parents to set limits unilaterally. Parents know that if they say, "You're not allowed to do that!" and their child replies, "I have a right to do it!" the family will become polarized in a power struggle. They are aware that two-sided negotiations, in which both parties take each other's needs and limits seriously, avoid destructive conflicts. These parents are less concerned with granting or refusing to grant permission than with establishing and maintaining respectful feelings in the family.

To create families in which all members thrive and develop in healthy ways, the focus needs to be on dialogue, not on "permission."

Families with Teenagers

The stage in the life of a family when children reach adolescence or enters puberty is surrounded by many myths and expectations.

Adolescence is a developmental period during which children have their second opportunity to know who they are and to become themselves (their first opportunity is during the age of independence, described in Chapter 1). Yet children are not always given this opportunity. For previous generations, adolescence was a time during which children could be shaped according to their parents' wishes. Many children succeeded in living up to their parents' visions and expectations, and some found success in life this way. Others went through life with feelings of inner emptiness and disappointment. To their perpetual dismay, the world did not reward their ability to adapt.

Other people were luckier in that they were able to withstand the pressures to adapt. Their sense of self-preservation triumphed over their parents' conformist wishes. Yet in many cases this successful break with their parents came at a high cost—years of constant and often fierce conflict.

The notion that adolescence in itself is the cause of conflicts with parents is a myth. Primarily, conflicts arise because parents lack the will or ability to recognize and engage with the unique and independent person that their child is in the process of becoming. Rather than acknowledge this drive toward individuality, parents often ascribe the conflicts to hormonal changes or variations (just as women's drive for individuality is mistakenly ascribed to hormones). In reality, the less parents are able to or desire to experience their child as an independent person, the fiercer and more destructive these conflicts become.

Ask adolecents all over the world and you will hear the same to statements: "My parents never listen" and "They just don't understand". This fact makes both the yungsters and their parents equaly lonely. This is not a law of nature it is a consequence of our parental behavior.

All family conflicts begin when two or more people want different things. Therefore there are always as many causes for a conflict as there are participants. As I said earlier, parents are responsible for the quality of interaction in a family, and this extends to the way in which conflicts happen, develop and are dealt with. Teenagers attempt to act like adults and expect to be treated as such. But they are not adults in the sense that they cannot assume responsibility for the quality of interaction with their parents.

During their teenage years, children who have hitherto cooperated to an extent that is beyond their ability often become uncooperative, and children whose integrity has been damaged become clearly destructive or self-destructive. In other words, the seeds that were sown during childhood come to fruition, and parents whose intentions were well intended often find themselves confronting children who seem very foreign to them.

Let me explain. When children reach the age of thirteen or fourteen, they begin to give us clear and competent feedback as to how they feel they have been treated for their entire lives. The feedback parents receive may be mainly positive or negative, but it will never be entirely positive or negative. Parents who discern an unambiguous message in the feedback they receive have mistakenly deluded themselves into thinking that everything revolves around them. That is, they are not paying attention to what their children are saying; they are simplifying and distorting what they hear.

When children reach the ages of thirteen to fifteen, they need to separate and free themselves from their parents. Children who don't accomplish this separation are unable to grow up to be independent, social, responsible, and critical adults. When children start to separate from their parents, they are not acting against us. They are acting for themselves. In a sense, they are continuing our work of parenting for themselves. It is a natural continuation of what we have done for them.

Many conflicts between parents and adolescents will diminish if parents follow the principles for interaction discussed so far. These principles can also help to create a foundation for a lifelong trusting relationship between parents and children. Such a relationship is not based on each member assuming a stereotyped role but on a friendship in which each member has equal dignity. I'd like to talk now about how we can liberate ourselves from our roles in ways that are less painful and more meaningful.

It's too Late for "Bringing Up" Children

As strange as it may seem, most parents violate their teenager's integrity by continuing to bring him up in a loving, well-meant, insistent way. There are two reasons for this:

1. Even the best and most loving parents "bring up" their children by exercising control over them, regulating them and demonstrating their superior knowledge to them. There is nothing wrong with that. In fact, these are the very qualities that make young children feel secure, as if they are being raised in competent hands. But when children get older, this way of relating to a child starts to chafe.

What made them feel secure when they were younger now feels like unwelcome interference. Their independence denied, they feel criticized and underestimated—and they are.

2. When children reach adolescence, it is too late to "bring them up." Children receive the most important tools for living from their parents during the first three to four years of their lives. Parents' contributions to their children's lives are still important during the next six to seven years. But by adolescence, peers, other adults, and children's own inner lives become the most important sources of inspiration.

All children make their parents aware that they no longer need bringing up when they say, more or less diplomatically, "I'll figure that out myself," or "Mind your own business!" Or, as my son once said, "The question is whether I still need my parents to involve themselves in that kind of thing." The longer it takes us to listen, the louder they speak.

When children speak this way, they are not sounding trumpets heralding the revolution. They are giving us well-meant, relevant pieces of advice that should signal us that we can now retreat from the front lines of parenthood and spend our excess time and energy on ourselves and each other.

When parents insist on continuing to "bring up" their teenagers, they convey two messages that no teenager wants to hear:

1. "I know what's good for you!" This infuriates teenagers because they are completely involved in discovering for themselves who they really are. Thus it is both provocative and meaningless to them when their parents pretend to know the answer.

2. "I am not satisfied with you the way you are!" It is unbearable for young people to be confronted with this kind of statement. For one thing, they do not yet know who they are beneath the varnish of their upbringing, and, second, they are not sure how much they like themselves.

At this point, the best thing parents can do for themselves— and for their child—is to lean back and enjoy the results of the hard work they have put in over the preceding years. And if they are not completely delighted with what they see, they must try to enjoy it all the same! What children need for the rest of their lives is parents who wholeheartedly support their attempts to discover who they are, and their efforts to be true to themselves.

Yet when confronted with the relative imperfections of their creations, most parents tend to do the opposite: they sit up and intensify their upbringing efforts in the hope that they can add the final touches. This is not possible—at least not for parents. **If you look at your teenager and do not se perfection – take a look in the mirror!**

Many parents who throw themselves into last-minute upbringing do so not so much out of conviction, but because they are at a loss about what to do with their love and feelings of responsibility. The very idea of doing nothing but enjoying their teenager seems irresponsible. They experience themselves as valuable to their child only when they are in action mode. In the process, they tend to forget that their actions prevent the young person from experiencing himself as a valuable part of his parents' lives. Instead he is put in a situation where he has to fight them

It is not just what we say to teenagers, but how we say it that fuels conflicts. Over generations, we have developed a language we use when addressing teenagers that is very different from the language we use when addressing other adults. The tone we use conveys superiority, condescension, and intrusion. At best it is friendly and embracing; at worst it is critically offensive. To the child, it says, "You have not yet become my equal." Generations ago, when adults felt this way about children, the words and tone they used were in consonance. Today, although many adults no longer agree with the subtext of the message, they still use the same language. As a result, the tone is jarring and the message contradictory.

This language is particularly and understandably objectionable to teenagers because it ignores their individuality. The best way out of this language trap is to ask yourself: "If I were having this conflict with my best adult friend, how would I express myself?" Your answer will guide you to a more constructive way of talking to your teenager.

What parents need to do is enter into a dialogue of equals with their children instead of dispensing knowledge. For many years, we have suffered from the misapprehension that it was necessary for children and young people to understand every word we say to them. But important parts of our messages get lost when we try to explain ourselves rather than express ourselves. Often it's the personal "music" that has an impact—not the specific words. Children—even very young children—need their parents to use a personal language with them when personal and interpersonal issues are being discussed. For their part, teenagers still need their parents to spar with them verbally—to react and express their opinions and attitudes. By resorting to an educational style of relating, we turn our backs on personal expression in an attempt to change or shape young people, and thereby the quality of our communication is reduced.

Here's an example. A fourteen-year-old girl introduces her boyfriend to her mother and later asks her, "Isn't he just adorable?"

One mother, who believes that she knows best, says, "Look at the way he behaves! He's certainly not the kind of boy for you!"

Another mother, who treats her daughter with equal dignity, says, "He's not quite my cup of tea, but I think it's lovely to see the way he makes your eyes light up."

Parents need to make themselves available to their teenagers without forcing themselves on them. Here are some comments a mother in this situation could make:

- "I have my own opinion about that. Would you like to hear it?"

- "This is something I feel I have to get involved in. Are you willing to listen to my point of view now?"

- "I'm concerned about what's happening to you, and I'd like to talk to you about it. Can we talk now?"

These comments are not polite in the usual social sense. Rather, they are expressions of respect for another person's sovereignty. I suggest that parents pause for ten seconds after such a statement in order to determine whether their teenager is perceiving their initiative as a violation or as an invitation to talk.

By speaking this way, the parent and teenager can rediscover each other's vulnerabilities and limits. It gives them the opportunity to reestablish respect for one another, a quality that often diminishes after many years of living together.

The best role for parents is the role of a "sparring-partner". In professional boxing this is a training partner who helps the upcoming champ get fit for fight. The job is to offer maximum resistance and do minimum damage.

Taking this role parents must avoid the use of power and instead seek influence by presenting their values, standpoint, and oppinions as personally and clearly as possible. In other words you are free to have your negative opinion about your sons girlfriend, but don't forbid him to see her.

PARENTS AND THEIR SENSE OF LOSS

When young people achieve their own freedom, many parents experience a sense of loss. It can be so painful that they are unable to face up to it until many years later. Others never do.

The vital and valuable role that parents have hitherto played in the life of their children has come to an end. They know their children still need them, but in attenuated ways. Their responsibility for their children has become a thing of the past.

Parents experience other losses as well:

* Closeness. Suddenly their children prefer to spend time with their friends or to sit alone in their room and listen to music.

* Power and control—both physical and emotional.

- Confidentiality. Children confide in friends, or boy-or girl friends.

For some parents these losses come as a shocking, tearful realization; other parents experience small clouds of sadness; and some feel relief. But all parents have to come to terms with this loss before they can change their position from the front lines to the rearguard of their children's lives.

Many parents are not aware (or have forgotten) that making this transition in relation to their children is necessary. That's why parents experience their loss as a surprise even when they have prepared themselves for it. Parents who have not faced up to this loss may feel a panicky or directly aggressive need to reassert themselves as child rearers and controlling authorities.

Here's a sample of dialogue between Lena, sixteen, and her parents. Lena has been invited to a party on Saturday evening by an acquaintance of her girlfriend.

"May I go to a party with Eva on Saturday? Her parents have given her permission."

"What kind of party is it? Who's giving the party, and where is it being held? Is it someone you know?"

"It's someone Eva knows. It's just an ordinary party."

"We don't know Eva's friends. Who are they, and how old are they?

Are the parents going to be at home?"

"No, I don't think so."

"You must know more than that! How do you expect us to trust you when you won't tell us about it? It's not unnatural, is it, for parents to take an interest in their children. Or perhaps it is these days?"

In this classic dialogue, Lena's parents have positioned themselves on parenting's front lines and have posted guards on all borders. Lena receives an unmistakable message: "We do not trust you, and we consider you to be completely incapable of assuming personal responsibility. We are not finished with you yet, my girl, but when we are, you will appreciate the fact that your parents did not accept indifference and carelessness!"

If Lena and teenagers in a similar situation are creative, they will soon learn how to give their parents the answers they want to hear, and stop telling them anything that even remotely resembles the truth. Sooner or later the parents will discover evidence of the fact that their children are not to be trusted, and the vicious circle will be perpetuated.

Here is an alternative approach to Lena's situation:

Lena begins: "I've been invited to a party on Saturday together with Eva and some of her friends. What do you think about that?"

"Is it a party you want to go to?"

"Yes! It sounds as if it's going to be fun, because there are a lot of people coming I don't know."

"Good. We haven't got any special plans for the weekend, so if that's what you want to do, we haven't got any objections. If you need any help getting there or want us to pick you up afterward, we'd like to know as soon as possible."

Or:

"We're planning to visit your Uncle Ian this weekend, and we'd like you to come. What do you think?"

"I'd much rather go to the party. A lot of new people are coming, and it sounds as if it's going to be fun. Is it just to visit Uncle Ian, or is something special happening?"

"It's just an ordinary visit. Well, think about it, and let us know what you decide. If you choose to go to the party, we'd like to know how you're getting there and how you will get home again, or where you're spending the night."

Or:

"You know very well that I'm not very keen on Eva and her friends, so I don't think you should go to that party!" "What have you got against Eva? She's perfectly nice and ordinary. It's just because you don't really know her."

"Maybe I don't know much about Eva. But the fact is, I don't like the idea of you going to that party with her. You don't have to do as I say, but that's the way I feel about that party."

Or:

"I can tell you right now, you're not going!"

As you can see, this dialogue isn't really about a party. It's about the ways in which Lena's parents can choose to exert their authority. For Lena, it's about the ways she can practice exercising her nascent sense of personal responsibility.

When teenagers ask for permission, it is important that parents play down their roles as legislators unless the situation involves their money or their property. Parents must be able to express their unreserved opinions as much as they want; by itself, this is not a misuse of power. The foundation for this kind of interaction should have been established years ago, through negotiations about social limits, during which children had the opportunity to develop their sense of personal responsibility.

Having this track record for negotiating puts parents in a position in which they are free to say: "I don't want you to go!" with such power that it implies, "Don't even think about staying away from that party just because I say so!"

This powerful statement forces a child to reflect. It says, "Now you know where I stand, and I assume that you will take it into consideration when you make your decision." If the nonverbal message is missing, children reject parents' overt advice or rebel against it. We should feel free to apply the same ethic to adult relationships. We must be free to express ourselves in order to make an impression on the other person, but not to misuse our emotional, physical, or financial power.

If Lena goes to the party, then her parents' role becomes that of rearguard or safety net. Suppose Lena looks sad on Sunday. Her mother can put an arm around her and say, "You look downhearted. Was it a bad party, Lena? Would you like to talk about it?"

If Lena's answer is no, her mother may have touched on the limits of Lena's private life. In this case, both parties will have to regain emotional equilibrium separately. If Lena says yes, she could be indicating her need for an adult's perspective and experience with such situations. But most probably, she needs her parents to listen and respond with a more personal comment. Only Lena's own words can restore her equilibrium and enable her to integrate her unpleasant experience.

Parents in the rearguard still have a very important task. All of us need to have loving and caring witnesses to our lives—preferably witnesses who are willing to show their concern for us when we need it, not when they have the need to make themselves feel useful.

Parents' Relationship with One Another

As teenagers discover their freedom, parents of teenagers experience their own important awakening. Their partnership as well as their individual lives are free to emerge from the shadows and to return to center stage. This, in turn, forces parents to adjust the way they balance their roles as partners and parents.

Interestingly, the lives of parents with teenage children are symmetrical with the lives of their children in several important ways:

- Parents and teens both go through a critical phase in their lives during which they focus on identity and the meaning of existence.

- They are in the process of freeing themselves from old roles and functions, as well as coping with the uncertainty that ac-companies such a role change, all the while trying to hang on to what is familiar.

- They must define themselves as individuals so that the family and other relationships can be adjusted in relation to their new phases of life.

In other words, **as children become adults, parents are given an opportunity to mature.**

Who Decides?

No matter how old their children are, parents have the same major responsibility: creating the family atmosphere, or the quality of interaction, in which every individual can grow and prosper. This responsibility cannot be delegated. What can be delegated, however, is some of the responsibility for the practical chores that are necessary for everyday family life, such as shopping and cleaning. In Scandinavia, parents naturally consider children responsible for a portion of these chores, but this is not the case in every country. In some societies boys are completely exempt and girls are more or less obliged; in others, even those mothers who work outside the home still shoulder total responsibility for family chores and don't imagine that the situation could be otherwise.

To my way of thinking, only one factor determines whether and to what extent young people should be expected to help with everyday family chores: it is solely a question of what the parents want them to do. If the issue of assigning chores is approached from any other perspective, conflicts will erupt.

Let me explain.

- If children are expected to do chores "of their own accord," one of two things usually happens: either the children assume too few chores and then parents become frustrated, or children assume too many chores and become overburdened, not knowing how much is expected of them.

- In families in which parents regard chores from a "moral" standpoint—"children ought to help their mother and father"—a slightly unpleasant atmosphere often pervades the household. When parents say, "You should" instead of "I want," they block the natural tendency we all have to take an interest in each other and what we each need and want. Instead these parents inspire feelings of spite and guilt.

- If chores become a sort of military duty, it is difficult to avoid court-martials or desertions.

  Parents who expect children to perform chores as a kind of repayment for the care lavished on them induce feelings of either guilt and/or permanent dissatisfaction in their children. Care can't be repaid in chores: these are completely incompatible currencies.

Yet the approach I advocate—having parents ask for help with certain chores—is difficult for many parents for several reasons. Often, parents have a harder time saying what they want than we might assume. Many parents take refuge from their discomfort by claiming that "it really shouldn't be necessary" to express their wishes—as if children should intuit what is needed without being asked. Some parents insist that they have asked for help thousands of times, whereas other parents take a shortcut and establish a set of stiff rules buttressed by control and sanctions.

Often those parents who have trouble asking for help with chores experienced similar difficulties when their children were younger, and these conflicts were never resolved. Most likely, the parents never took themselves or their demands seriously and therefore developed a double-dealing relationship with their children: after asking their children to clean up five or six times in the course of a day, they subsequently ended up performing the task themselves.

Other families struggle over chores because children were raised to be overly responsible. This tendency is common in families in which one parent is sick, depressed, or disabled. Children feel resentful when they are taken to task for failing to do the dishes—a trivial chore, to their way othinking—despite the years they devoted to the emotional and physical care of an ill or absent parent.

Whatever the cause of the dispute, parents need to negotiate household chores with their children, expressing their limits and demands in direct, personal language. For example, parents could say to their teenager, "We have talked it over, and we have decided that we want you to have responsibility for taking out the garbage [or some equivalent chore]. What do you think about that?"

If the child asks, "Why do I have to do that?" the answer is: "Because that's the way we want it. You don't necessarily have to take out the garbage, but we want you to contribute some practical help to the life of the family."

If the child says, "No, that's unreasonable! How can I manage all the other things I have to do?" the answer is:

"O. K. Let's hear what you think is reasonable."

"Well, I don't know. It's just too much. Can't we just scale back a little?"

"That's possible, but you'll have to make your own suggestion. Now you have an idea of what we think are reasonable demands in relation to what we need as a family, and now we'd like to hear what you think."

It is vitally important that parents and children assume their share of the responsibility as the negotiation continues. This may mean that parents will first need to erase the following standard replies from their automatic parental answering machine:

- "Now, listen here! It's not unreasonable that. . ."

- "If it's going to cause so much trouble, perhaps weought to have a talk about adjusting your allowance."

- "It's not unusual that children of your age. . ."

- "Now don't be silly! You don't really mean that your mother. . ."

- "If we think about what it costs us. . ."

- "When I was your age. . ."

(The list is much longer than stated here, but additional comments are neither less embarrassing nor more effective.)

As mentioned earlier, the chores children will assume vary from one family to another. No one task has more inherent value than any other. How should chores be assigned? Children can be asked which chores they'd prefer, although for most healthy and active teenagers, doing the dishes, cleaning, and cooking rank very low on their list of what is important in life. If they are moved to do chores at all, it is usually out of a "sudden impulse." Of course, the performance of household chores cannot depend on spontaneous desire.

In negotiating which chores are to be done by teenagers, the way in which the family decision-making process unfolds is more important than the actual decisions that are reached. It is better to take plenty of time to reach decisions than to forge hurried compromises in order to establish domestic peace. Also it is better to ensure that both parties are taken seriously than to cut off discussions by proposing a "fair" solution.

In many families, the issue of chores is significant because when the children reach their teenage years, they are old enough to refuse to cooperate. Until this point, many parents have not had to seriously confront the quality of the family's decision-making process. They enlisted their children's cooperation by creating halfhearted compromisesand evoking a sense of "duty." (Relying on this method gradually but inevitably undermines the relationship they have with their children, but the degree of erosion is often not revealed until the children leave home.)

By the time children become teenagers, however, they are old enough to say no when asked to cooperate. Some children refuse to fulfill agreements and obligations without any real explanation. Teenagers respond this way not only in families in which the children have been brought up rigidly, but also in seemingly flexible families. In fact, many flexible parents base their demand for flexibility, consideration, and social responsibility on strong moral principles; in this sense, they are rigid. Often children have experienced this rigidity as a burden or a barrier to closeness for years, yet their reaction to their experience of the family dynamic is only revealed when the children are old enough to refuse to be involved.

What happens when children refuse, and neither arguments nor sensible conversations improve the situation? In my view, children who don't cooperate are telling us that the family expects too much cooperation from its members. Therefore these children must be officially excused from all duties in the family for an indefinite period of time.

Why? The child's refusal signals that her sense of personal and social responsibility is seriously and dangerously out of balance. If this was not the case—if her integrity was not being threatened—she wouldn't need to react in such aradically asocial manner. To reestablish her social responsibility, she needs to regain her personal responsibility, sincethis is a prerequisite for developing a real sense of social responsibility.

To many adults, this sounds simple but highly provocative. But it is the only method of which I am aware that guarantees success. More important, its effectiveness is based on a sound ethical foundation. From my experience, it takes an average of six to eight months before rebellious children begin to act in helpful ways around the house. Depending on the extent to which parents are able to welcomethis helpfulness and refrain from exploiting it, the child's social responsibility within the framework of the family will become firmly established after approximately one to one and a half years. But perhaps the most significant achievement is that the child is developing her personal responsibility and thus no longer needs to act defiantly.

The healing process I recommend is difficult for both parties. Children don't like not contributing to the family (don't be fooled by the fact that your child's first reaction to no longer having any chores may well be, "Cool!"). As for parents, they must think and act in ways that are completely opposite to what they have learned to regard as sacred.

But the process cannot be avoided. Parents need to use this time to face up to the fact that their moral code may have lacked foundation. This does not mean that theirmoral concepts were "wrong," but rather that over time these concepts became automatic, and now they need to be imbued with substance.

Parents must be decisive. They are the captains of the ship. Whether the ship reaches harbor safely, without mutiny, depends on how responsibly they use their power, and how willing they are to alter the speed and course according to the nature of the wind and the crew. The basis for setting the course is the fact, that any human being living in a group or community without making a contribution to it's wellfare looses her or his personal dignity.

When Success is almost Achieved

Some children seem to be doing fine, but then they take a destructive path. They turn to crime or addiction, or they resort to other courses of action that their parents have tried to inoculate them against.

Developments like these sorely tempt parents to reassert and intensify their roles as upbringers—so desperate are they to put an end to their child's self-destructive behavior. But even though the pain feels unbearable and their desire to seize control is overwhelming, parents need to acknowledge that it is too late to achieve the desired ends. In fact, such attempts only serve to make the situation worse for both parents and children. Once the initial paralysis and panic have begun to wear off, parents need to do three things:

1. Share their feelings of guilt, self-reproach, and blame with each other and with other adults—not with their child—so that they can vent these feelings and concentrate their energy on their responsibility and the future.

2. Be direct and personal when talking with their child. They need to take responsibility for their own feelings and reactions and not attempt to assume the role of therapist, police officer, judge, or religious figure. Remember, the child's self-destructive

behavior is not directed toward his parents. It is his attempt to undermine his own human dignity.

3. Assume the responsibility for obtaining help for the family. It doesn't matter whether the parents first turn to a good friend of the family, a teacher, a priest, or aprofessional family therapist. The most important thing is that the whole family—including other children—receives help. Every member of the family feels like an accessory, and every member shares the responsibility. Remember, however, that public services and private counseling can be effective only to the extent that the family determines to examine itself and change the way its members interact.

When a young person starts to act self-destructively, it is because of many interrelated factors—including friends, the social and economic condition of his society and the family, the culture, and the policy toward children and youths in the local community. And then, of course, there is the family. Irrespective of how powerful the other factors may appear, we as parents must face up to the fact that something about our connection with our children made them vulnerable. Something we gave them, or neglected to give them, made it impossible for their self-esteem and self-responsibility to develop. Although we did the best we could, quite innocently, we let them down.

Therefore if we want to make an important contribution to our children's lives, we need to acknowledge our share of the responsibility—for the sake of our own peace of mind, and for our children. We must take responsibility on two fronts: that destructive processes existed within the family, and that we need to replace them with constructive processes. If we shirk this responsibility, then our children will internalize our failing as guilt, which will increase their vulnerability.

There are two additional reasons for obtaining outside help. No parents can objectively grasp or perceive the interactive process in their own families. (My colleagues and I, who are psychologists and family therapists, can bear witness to the fact that this advice also applies to so-called experts.) Only through outside help can parents become aware of the destructive processes that exist and have existed in the family.

In the years between the onset of puberty and the start of adult life, young people have a very difficult time altering their self-destructive behavior without help from outside the family. They are on the verge of completing their development according to their genetic inheritance and their growth in the family. They have managed to maintain a balance between fulfilling their own needs and their urge to cooperate with their parents, to the extent that this was possible in their family. In other words, they have completed fifteen years of hard work, and the fruits of this labor are just beginning to emerge.

Despite their sometimes raw and rough surface, teenagers are as vulnerable as newly emerged butterflies drying their wings in the sun. When the transformation is almost complete, some of them start to do destructive and self-destructive things. If parents or other adults make them feel guilty, they freeze in their behavioral patterns, and the self-destructiveness becomes almost impossible to stop. On the other hand, if parents are prepared to assume an active, personal share of the responsibility, teenagers can slowly begin to rebuild their self-esteem—and ultimately they will treat themselves better.

FAMILY

Families are more diverse than ever before. In this chapter, I will focus on the nuclear family—two adults and their children.

I will try to enumerate a number of fruitful principles adults can follow as they try to strengthen the bonds within their families. This is an important goal, because, as I have also learned through my therapeutic work, the old model of the marital relationship—in which inequity exists between the partners—is close to extinction.

For hundreds of years, men and women have turned to marriage to provide social stability, security, and acceptance. Clearly, unmarried women were in a more insecure social situation than unmarried men were. This is still the case in many countries. But, for the most part, people in the Western world have developed completely new demands and expectations of the role that marriage and partnership will play in their lives.

Marriage or simply living together as adults has become an existential choice for modern men and women. What I mean by this is that we no longer look to marriage to provide us with social acceptability or security. The main thing we want from marriage is to create meaningful relationships that are emotionally and spiritually fulfilling

This is an exciting development. Human dignity is much more important than ever before. The importance of making dignity our new priority forms the basis of this chapter.

When I compare my experience of doing therapy with couples from the various countries and cultures with which I am familiar, two things become clear. First, the deep conflicts that exist in love-based relationships are universal. Whatever cultural and religious differences exist are superficial in comparation.

Second, I have found that the traditional model for a "good marriage," which was based on the unequal relationship between men and women, is becoming outdated. Am I being too optimistic? (As an old friend and colleague once said, "When you have a hammer, everything starts looking like a nail."). I hope not.

Beginning with this new focus on human dignity, I will attempt to formulate some general principles according to which adults can live together in the spirit of equal partnership. The chapter will not give specific or concrete advice—it is pointless to replace old rules with new rules—but rather it will map out a blueprint for experimentation and transition. In my experience, the principle of equal dignity requires deep respect for individual differences, and any attempt to generalize or oversimplify should be taken with a grain of salt.

DIFFERENCE

When two people meet each other, fall in love, and decide to live their lives together, the differences between them are far greater than the similarities. They know this, but it is as if their love dulls their senses and removes them to a fan-tasy world. In other words, they fool themselves into believing that loving each other and creating a life together depends on being as much alike as possible. In the first phase of living together, they attempt to achieve this uniformity by surrendering themselves for the benefit of unity; somewhat later they start to desire or demand that the other person sacrifice a part of him- or herself as a token of love and proof of dedication to the relationship. This is the eternal and universal pattern. It cannot be prevented, only interrupted.

Yet when we talk about parents, two clear differences immediately come to mind. First is the fact that they are most often of opposite sexes. The other is that they have different personalities.

I think of our "personalities" as the sum of our different strategies for survival, which have been shaped by the opportunities and limitations that were accorded to us in the family and culture in which we were raised. Our overall strategy for survival is an expression of the way in which we learned to deal with the conflict between integrity and cooperation so that it became as bearable as possible for ourselves, and as acceptable as possible for our parents.

Our strategy for survival is always partly self-destructive. Regardless of what we remember about our childhood, we all received certain wounds and developed a number of unhealthy ways of treating ourselves. Some of us sought refuge in solitude, some tried to fuse with our parents, and others found more or less comfortable ways of existing somewhere between those extremes.

It's important to remember that our self-destructive behavior is always destructive to those closest to us and to ourrelationship with them. As soon as they begin to love us, they open themselves to us and become vulnerable. Because we have lived with our self-destructive tendencies for a clong time, we often become immune to the pain these tendencies cause us, or we resign ourselves to it. But our selfdestructive behavior and its consequences make a very strong impression on our partners and children, who have not known us so long. The strategy for survival that was appropriate in our family of origin is very seldom a strategy we want to try in our next family. We make a mistake when we equate our initial strategy for survival with a strategy for life.

How can we transform our strategy for survival into a strategy for life? We need two ingredients—the love we receive from others combined with our desire to be as valuable as possible to them in their lives. And then we have to work hard at the transformation.

If we start a family for the first time before we reach the age of thirty or thirty-five, we know neither the other person nor ourselves. We know only our two personalities, which, as I have explained, mainly consist of our individual strategies for survival. We don't dwell on our differences. Being in love imbues us with a sense of well-being, both for ourselves and for each other, so it is natural that we do not think about the fact that we will soon have to start developing and changing ourselves.

For previous generations, the culture demanded not that people develop but that they adapt. When people joined together to form families, the new families demanded what one's family of origin demanded: self-sacrifice. They had to give up themselves for the sake of others and for the sake of "peace" within the family.

In the modern family, in which relationships are based on equal dignity, the demands are quite different: a constructive relationship with a partner and children demands that we are willing to develop ourselves as human beings not because of conditions imposed by other members of the family, but because they are in pain.

Because our strategies for survival are most often quite unique, the amount of time we need to develop and the opposition we encounter along the way will also be unique. Our adult partner can be more or less patient, and more or less sensitive to our pain. Children, however, show very little inhibition. They assure us, in very clear ways, that we are perfect and all-powerful. The more determined we are to develop aspects of our own personalities, the less selfdestructive our children will become. Reciprocity replaces one-sidedness.

Many couples view their differences as a source of inspiration. Yet when we become parents and the development of new life hangs quite literally in the balance, we often experience these differences between us as more of a burden than an inspiration. Sometimes it's helpful to remind each other that when two adults become parents, the most fortunate possess, between the two of them, approximately one third of the experience, insight, and know-how necessary to do a more or less competent job of raising their child. This knowledge arises from what they learn from each other, and what their children teach them by way of the competent feedback they supply as they grow.

It is in the nature of the learning process that conflicts will arise. Thus we need to determine how conflicts can be seen in a constructive way, as opposed to using them to establish who is in the "right."

Let's study an example familiar to every new parent:

She: It can't be right that she cries every time you change her. Why do you always have to be so rough with her?

He: When she needs changing, she needs changing. You may have time to play with her for hours on end every time you do it, but she might just as well learn that some things need to be done and gotten over with!

She: Yes, but you can see for yourself that it's not pleasant for her.

He: I'm not talking about what's pleasant or not. I'm saying that some things just have to be done, and then there's time to play afterward. What about when she is at the day-care center? Do you think they have time to pay special attention to her?

This conflict is classic in the sense that two different attitudes—the masculine and feminine—are on a collision course. Determining with whom we sympathize is the least important aspect of the conflict. The most important thing is that these two people are condemning each other's way of doing things: "Your way is too rough!" "Yours is unrealistic!"

Suppose the conflict had developed another way:

She: It can't be right that she cries every time you change her. Why do you always have to be so rough with her?

He: It's possible that I don't do things your way, but this is my way of doing it! O. K. ?

She: O. K., then. . .

This version is an example of what happens when respect for personal difference is reduced to a phrase. On the surface, it appears that this couple has reached a compromise, but in fact their dialogue is characterized by a lack of contact that typifies our sense of individualism. The father is alone with his attitude, the mother with her concern—while the baby continues to cry. The conflict has been stripped of expressive language and feelings, but it is far from having been defused.

If the dialogue between these two parents is to be meaningful and constructive, it must be personal and relate to them. There is some justification for claiming that attitudes are personal and that discussions about attitudes can be constructive; but the prerequisite for these conversations is that they be purely intellectual, and that is rarely the case when the subject under discussion is the ways in which parents live together and treat their children.

In this instance, since the conflict is about personal pain and frustration, the parents need to use personal language.

She: Listen. It upsets me that Emma always cries when you change her. Can we talk about it now?

He: Yes, all right. Have I done something wrong again!?

She: I don't know whether it's wrong. I just know that it upsets me every time, and that I feel like going in and helping you to get along better with her. I don't know whether it would annoy you if I interfered, and that's why I have to talk to you about it now. . . I think what I most need to hear is how you feel about it.

He: I don't see it as a problem. I would prefer it if she laughed all the time, but it has to be done.

She: Perhaps we're not that different after all. Would you like to hear some good suggestions?

He: No, not really. . . . I just don't know whether I can do it any differently. . . . in my own way, I mean.

For most conflicts that unfold like this one, it would be helpful if the couple stopped talking at this point. Both parties have succeeded in listening to each other and taking each other's limits seriously. They have made an impression on each other instead of trying to convince each other; remember—the "musical" quality of the conversation is more important for the well-being of the whole family than reaching a possible conclusion or agreement. We often imagine that we'll develop more quickly if conflicts reach a conclusion, but this is rarely the case. Often the quest for resolution brings personal development to a standstill. It is possible that Emma will continue to be frustrated and angry with her father for weeks or months to come, but it is much better for her to live with her feelings than to have her parents use her as a weapon in their power struggle.

Let's return for a moment to Emma's mother's first attempt to alter the destructive interaction in her family: "It can't be right that she cries every time you change her. Why do you always have to be so rough with her?" What she is really saying is: "You are doing it in the wrong way, and you are too rough with her."

Her opening remark is a good example of how content is always less important than process whenever two people interact. Let us assume that she is right in her observation—that the interaction between father and daughter is, in fact, inappropriate because he treats the baby without sympathy and understanding, as if she was a task that had to be accomplished. Notice, however, that the tone and form of the mother's comment is just as insensitive and offensive as the behavior she accuses her husband of. Her allegation thereby lacks credibility. Instead of solving a problem in her family, she doubles it. Furthermore, the way she cares for her daughter will suffer if she does not figure out how to combine her care for her baby with consideration for her partner.

Paradoxically, she speaks to her partner in this way because that was how her parents spoke to her when she was a child needing correction. Her whole organism recalls the pain—that's why she speaks up for her daughter—but it is only a matter of time before she starts to treat her daughter in the same way. She, like all of us, acts destructively out of good intentions. But when parents begin a family, it is their responsibility to attempt to rise above the past. They must attempt to leave behind the fruitless actions and attitudes that arose from the love they felt for their own parents.

SHARED LEADERSHIP

There are many models of family leadership. In contemporary Europe alone, some families have at their helm a domineering, patriarchal, domestic tyrant; others, a gentle, resolute Earth Mother. Some parents see themselves as a democratic duo who make all decisions together; in other families, respectful coleaders carve out carefully defined fiefdoms in which to exercise personal power. Other parents fight bitterly over every square inch of territory and ounce of power. And some families conceive of a partnership in which each parent has equal dignity.

These models of leadership are based on two premises. The first is that women and men are equal in terms of their social, political, and economic lives. The second is the idea that men and fathers should share an active responsibility for the everyday running of the home; that is, they need to be emotionally integrated into the family, and play an active, daily part in looking after the children. In light of the historical tradition of the family in Europe, this is a revolutionary concept.

Men and fathers have always had important areas of responsibility both within and in relation to the family, but only rarely have they been included in the ongoing, rhythmic pattern of daily life shared by mothers and children. In fact, as recently as the mid-1930s, Danish child-rearing experts recommended that children eat before their fathers returned home from work. It was seen as undesirable that the head of the household and family provider should partake of his main meal of the day in the company of young children!

Shared leadership is characterized by the fact that both parents are capable of assuming all the necessary roles required in the family and are willing to have their roles overlap when required. Even if, over the course of time, couples who live together establish ways of sharing responsibilities according to their interests and talents, it is an arrangement with specified areas of responsibility. For example, in some families, the man looks after the fields, the animals, and the machines, while the woman cares for the children, the house, and the garden. This arrangement, with specified areas of responsibility, can undoubtedly be characterized by great dignity and respect, but that is not an example of shared leadership.

Furthermore, shared leadership arises from the belief that both adults have equal rights with regard to decision making, and that decisions are either made together or by the partner who is most competent in a particular area. This arrangement differs from democratically led families in which everything is discussed and decided upon jointly. Also decisions made by one partner are supported by the other, even in those cases in which there is a difference of opinion. In families in which the leadership is shared, disagreement and differences of opinion or priority often take the form of feedback after decisions have been made, and are not elements in a struggle for power. The goal of negotiations is not to be proven right, but to make an impression and to be taken seriously.

In terms of parenting, shared leadership takes as its starting point the idea that both parents and children have different limits and different needs. It is not based on parents agreeing about limits and rules, but on the principle that an individual has the right to be taken seriously. This strengthens the family and the quality of the interpersonal relations.

Such a family can be referred to as a "post-democratic family", in which the quality of decision making is accorded more importance than the decision itself, and in which minorities are involved instead of marginalized. An increasing number of families are developing this kind of leadership.

One of the problems they face, however, is that they are pioneers. None of society's institutions—whether political or private—offers role models. This is one of the many reasons why shared leadership cannot be established in a linear fashion in individual families. Instead, it develops as a slow process that will vary based on the development of each member of the family.

Partnership and Parentship

In the past, when a couple had their first child, the husband traditionally maintained his career and took care of his work. He was merely expected to add being a father to his other roles and shoulder an increased obligation to support the family. When a woman became a mother, her status underwent a more radical change. This often entailed giving up her independent, feminineidentity for the sake of her maternal role, which would remain the same throughout her life—with the assumption, later on, of the grandmotherly role.

These roles still exist in many parts of the world; the idea that family scripts could be rewritten is relatively new. Only in certain countries have women started to regardtheir traditional role as socially and existentially limiting. Often, somewhat later, men have begun to question their role as well.

Yet the rigidity of the mother and father roles is not merely historically determined. The whole experience of having a child is such an overwhelming event and creates such an enormous emotional upheaval that the majority of couples soon begin to identify themselves and each other with these particular roles. Some people actually stop using each other's given names and start calling one another "Father" and "Mother."

For the majority of us, parentship suddenly takes up so much of our lives that our partnership tends to fade into the background for a number of years. Theoretically, it can be argued that this weakening of the parental partnership—with its concomitant sense of loss and frustration—is also disadvantageous to children. There is one particular aspect of the partnership of parents that is of great importance for parentship and for the possibilities that parents have of discussing and solving conflicts that concern their children: partners need to be able to talk to one another as man and woman, as friends and lovers, as two people who have theirown personal identities. If a woman dislikes the way in which her husband helps their son with his homework, it is important that she approach her husband as his friend and partner, and not as her child's mother. If a wife feels anxious about her teenage daughter's activities outside the house, it is important that the husband hear her worries as her husband and partner, and not as his daughter's father. Parental roles are best suited for interaction with children. In interaction between adults, it is important that adults represent themselves.

This approach is not just important for keeping the friendship and the erotic sides of a relationship alive; paradoxically, it also ensures that we continue to develop as parents and human beings. If when we talk to each other about our relationship to our children we always do so in our roles as father and mother, then children are always at the center of our conversations, which inevitably are about what children do or do not do. To develop as human beings so that we can meet our children in the most constructive way possible, we must talk about ourselves with each other. Naturally, our children can serve as the starting point and inspiration for these conversations, but they should not be the perpetual objects.

It is easy to forget this principle; that's why we need each other's help to remember. Apart from being mothers and fathers, we are also individual women and men with our own experiences, feelings, needs, histories, and dreams, which exist independent of our parental roles. We can help to remind each other of this reality by going to the movies together, taking weekend vacations, and going out to dinner. But it is also a good idea to be on the alert for those conversations that have gone on for more than an hour and that have been focused exclusively on the children.

Occasionally I meet parents who believe that the only way for them to continue to develop as individuals is to find possibilities for growth outside the home. This belief starts in motion a vicious cycle. Parents experience themselves as growing less important to each other and less central to each other's lives. This happens not because they are unimportant, but because they can't imagine a different scenario. Some people, on the other hand, feel that seeking new experiences outside the family is a threat. But in reality, the real threat to a marriage is a couple's lack of awareness of the possibilities that exist for inspiring their partnership.

From my experience, there are very few things that have as positive an impact on our individual existence as having a loving, committed and existentially inspiring partnership. In a certain sense, it is only recently that families have chosen this goal as a priority. A great many families still exist in which the most conspicuous factor is the amount of unused human potential.

Reciprocity is Equal Respect

I would imagine that human beings have always experienced a sense of wonder, reverence, and responsibility, when first confronted with the new life they have created. The desire and urge to protect and love the child, and the will to give him or her a good life, unfold like a sunrise within us. Even those of us who had an unhappy childhood and are not happy in our present lives feel this urge.

But this urge to give is reciprocal. Children feel it in relation to us. This is a concept we need to learn. Children allow us to feel of value by virtue of their own existence, which in turn allows them to experience themselves as being of value.

This is only possible when we learn to restrain our selfcenteredness and to recognize our children's personal competence as a gift from them—a gift that they don't realize they are offering until we accept it. If we fail to learn this, they grow up believing that they have no other value except what can be expressed through grades in school and social success. This is not just painful for them and stigmatizing for our contact with them; it also does not help them become more productive members of society.

Oddly, we have always been aware of the gift of their competence, though traditionally we have acknowledged it only half of the time. When children behave nicely and develop smoothly, we interpret these traits as signs of our own value and competence, and respond by telling our children how "good" they are. On the other hand, when children are uncontrollable, naughty, frustrated, and destructive, we react by thinking that it must be because of something we have failed to do, thereby acknowledging our own partial incompetence. But we have always believed that the way forward was to *give* more—more upbringing, more love, more restrictions, more corporal punishment, more control.

There are two explanations for this. The first is cultural: we tend to do what everyone else does. The second reason is that when we feel that we are not of as much value in our relations with other people as we would like to be, we react aggressively by becoming irritable, frustrated, angry, and violent. And in those cases in which there is much at stake—in relation to our children and partners—our reactions are strongest. We question their value for us and in this way we reproach them because we do not feel ourselves to be of sufficient value.

This happens when children are small and stumble over something on the sidewalk. We pull their arm and react with an irritable, "Look where you're going!" When our five-year-old comes in crying for the third time that day with a scraped knee, we say, "You must learn to look where you're going!" When teachers inform us that our children do not meet their demands or expectations, we become angry with them or our children, or both. When our marriageis at a standstill or is crumbling, we find fault with our partner; when we cannot cope with life, we blame our parents or society. The only time we don't do this is if we have learned to turn our anger inward, toward ourselves, and to drown ourselves in feelings of guilt, depression, and selfreproach.

In relation to children, we have now learned that we must listen to our children, recognize them as competent, and learn from them, thereby becoming as valuable to them as we want to be. When our children's behavior makes us feel less than valuable, then it is nearly always because we are—that is, prior to the particular conflict, we were unable to convert our loving feelings into loving behavior, and our good intentions into fruitful interaction.

This is not a situation that we can change immediately by taking action. We can only open ourselves toward our children and attempt to decode their spontaneous or (out of loyalty to us) delayed feedback. Children do not attempt to teach us anything; neither do they employ educational theory. They simply live together with us and let us know how they experience it.

The majority of us develop so slowly as human beingsthat we do not cease to become angry or irritated until long after our children have become adults. Learning to change our perception is difficult and takes time. But there is nothing wrong with taking our time as long as we do not persist with the illusion that the fault lies with our children.

The father of a violently uncontrollable seven-year-old boy once looked me straight in the eye and asked, with exactly the same kind of despair and defiance in his voice that his son had inherited, "Is it really necessary to think so much about what you say to a boy of his age? My parents never damn well said anything but, NO!"

I do not think that any of my readers will be surprised to learn that my answer was, "Yes!"

Not only must we clean our traditional parental language from ways and words which are violating the personal integrity of our children. As part of implementing a new paradigm we must take the next logical step in the development of the human psyche – the art of dialouge – which requires a new vocabulary and a determination to meet our children i ways that will make it possible for us to discover *who* they are instead of defining who and what they should become.